Matt Tebbutt

weekend

Matt Tebbutt

weekend

**Eating at Home: From Long Lazy
Lunches to Fast Family Fixes**

Photography by Chris Terry

Hardie Grant

QUADRILLE

INTRODUCTION 7

Friday Night 10

Breakfast and Brunch 48

Lunch and BBQ 76

Saturday Night 120

Sunday Lunch 162

Desserts 192

INDEX 216
ACKNOWLEDGEMENTS 223

Introduction

My weekends are usually an even split of work and play – although I'm fortunate in that my work often feels a lot like play. Time spent in my home kitchen is always leisurely and fun; cooking should be relaxing and enjoyable, not a stressful experience.

In our house, there's usually music on in the background, a full glass of something chilled on the side and a fridge full of exciting ingredients. An optimistic friend of mine often says, 'If life got any better I couldn't handle it,' and I agree. I do recognize how lucky I am to be able to eat, drink and be merry, without too many woes and worries. I'm hoping that through this book, and by sharing my favourite recipes and entertaining ideas, I can spread the excitement I feel about a weekend spent cooking great dishes and enjoying them with friends and family.

The best home-cooked food is a celebration of simple ingredients done well, and at weekends there's more time and scope to try new things. There's time for quick-fix snacks, time for breakfasts so big they'll keep you going until suppertime and time for going all-out to impress, with long lunches and fancy dinners.

As with all good food, the best place to start is with great shopping. The better the quality of the ingredients, the less you have to fuss over them. We all like to experiment a bit with food, adding a bit of this, that and the other – but if you want simply grilled fish or a great steak sandwich, then buy and source your ingredients well.

There's a mistaken belief that chefs make absolutely everything from scratch. That's not the case. When I need a quick mayonnaise, I'll grab the jar from the fridge. If I need tomato sauce, it'll be the one we all know! There's nothing wrong with a well-stocked cupboard full of bottles and jars of ready-made stuff. They're a great starting point when you want to knock out something quick and tasty for a weekend treat.

In the recipes that follow, I'm going to walk you through some chilled and easy Friday night suppers, some lazy late breakfasts and full-blown brunches. Then we'll move along through casual weekend lunches and barbecue feasts for friends, then push-the-boat-out Saturday night dinners. We'll linger over the traditional Sunday lunch fodder for the grown-ups, and finish up with something sweet and a little bit decadent.

Weekends are all about a rolling conveyor belt of great food, one meal gliding into the next, punctuated by a slightly different tone to keep up the excitement and enthusiasm for each meal.

The recipes in this book are of two sorts: easily achievable or slightly aspirational. I hope to introduce you to some easy, fun recipes that you may not have tried before, as well as some dishes that are more challenging, but impressive enough to place in the centre of the table for guests.

Serving good food should be a means of celebration – a time to gather friends and family around a table to chat, eat and enjoy. The weekend starts here.

10

The end of the working week means looking forward to relaxing and having some fun. This translates into fuss-free fodder – dishes that are not too complicated, yet a bit more special than the usual weekday fare.

Weekends should have a 'start-as-you-mean-to-go-on' kind of vibe. Friday night is the time to kick back and make your weekend plans, wine or a beer in hand, and give in to the excitement of having a couple of days to indulge in some fun before the Monday morning, back-to-school reality kicks in.

I've pulled together some recipes that don't involve too much effort or pre-planning, and with minimal clearing up. I've also gone for a few spicy, chilli-fuelled dishes – because who doesn't like a curry on a Friday night?

Friday Night

PORTUGUESE CHICKEN, CORIANDER AND GARLIC SOUP

Serves 2

I first had a version of this soup in an unassuming little restaurant just outside Lisbon that only served very traditional Portuguese dishes. I didn't realize how tasty such a simple soup could be. Bold herbs, plenty of garlic and a great stock, all enriched with a broken egg yolk – proper rustic, country food at its very best.

For the soup
500ml (17fl oz) really deep, rich, fresh chicken stock
Stalks from 1 small bunch of coriander (cilantro), chopped (about 4 tbsp)
2 garlic cloves, thinly sliced
1 tsp black peppercorns
1 bay leaf
2 slices of stale sourdough bread, lightly toasted, cut into small chunks
1 x 120g (4oz) cooked chicken breast, thinly sliced
Sea salt and freshly ground black pepper

For the poached eggs
2 medium free-range eggs

To serve
Leaves from 1 small bunch of coriander
1 small green chilli, deseeded and finely chopped
2 tbsp olive oil

To make the soup, gently simmer the chicken stock, coriander (cilantro) stalks, garlic, peppercorns and bay leaf in a saucepan for 30 minutes.

Bring a sauté pan of water to the boil, then reduce the heat to a gentle simmer. Carefully crack in the eggs and poach gently for 2–3 minutes, or until cooked to your liking (but, let's face it, you want the yolks to be runny!). Remove using a slotted spoon and drain on a plate lined with paper towel. Set aside somewhere warm if possible.

Arrange the toasted bread chunks and chicken slices in the bottom of warmed serving bowls. Strain the hot stock into the bowls (reserve the sliced garlic but discard the other flavourings). Carefully add a poached egg to each bowl and season with sea salt and freshly ground black pepper.

Garnish with the reserved garlic slices, fresh coriander leaves and chopped green chilli. Drizzle over the olive oil to serve, before cracking open that glorious yolk.

Serves 4

1–1½ litres (35–52fl oz) light
 chicken stock
3cm (1¼in) piece root ginger,
 unpeeled and sliced
2 garlic cloves, sliced
2 tbsp Thai fish sauce
4 lime leaves
1 whole star anise
2 red chillies, sliced
1 green chilli, sliced
100g (3½oz) fine vermicelli rice
 noodles
4 x 150g (5½oz) fillets skinless
 salmon, thinly sliced
2 tbsp coriander (cilantro) leaves
2 tbsp mint leaves
2 pineapple rings (I used tinned),
 cut into 5mm (¼in) dice
1 pak choi, cored and leaves
 separated
2 spring onions (scallions), sliced

This is a delicious, super-quick, comforting dish with that all-important kick of chilli. Perfect for a fast, fiery Friday night supper.

Pour the chicken stock into a large saucepan and add the ginger, garlic, Thai fish sauce, lime leaves, star anise and chillies, bring to the boil, then turn down the heat and simmer for 20 minutes.

Put the vermicelli noodles in a heatproof bowl, pour over boiling water to cover and allow the noodles to sit for 5–10 minutes, or until as soft as you like them (I prefer mine to retain a bit of bite). Drain in a sieve or colander.

Spoon the drained noodles into serving bowls and add the slices of raw salmon, herbs, pineapple, pak choi and spring onions (scallions). Pour over the aromatic chicken stock and leave to stand for 5 minutes before serving, to lightly poach the salmon.

HOT AND SOUR SOUP

Serves 4

For the broth
2 tbsp vegetable oil
2 boneless, skinless chicken
    thighs, cut into thin strips
6 small shiitake mushrooms,
    thinly sliced
2 garlic cloves, finely chopped
2 tsp finely chopped root ginger
1 litre (35fl oz) chicken stock
1 medium free-range egg, beaten
1 tsp toasted sesame oil, plus
    extra to serve
2 tsp soy sauce
1 tsp chilli oil
1–2 tbsp black vinegar or rice
    wine vinegar

To garnish
4 spring onions (scallions),
    thinly sliced
1 red chilli, deseeded and
    finely chopped

This is my go-to quick-fix supper. If you have a fully stocked store cupboard, it doesn't require many other ingredients. The chicken can be substituted for leftover ham or Sunday's roast pork. Delicious and comforting.

Heat a large saucepan over a medium heat and add the oil. Once hot, add the chicken strips and cook until golden brown, about 4–5 minutes. Remove from the pan, cover and keep warm.

Add the mushrooms, garlic and ginger to the hot pan and cook, stirring, for 2–3 minutes. Pour in the stock and cook for 10–15 minutes.

In a bowl, whisk the egg, sesame oil, soy sauce, chilli oil and vinegar.

Tip the egg mixture into the broth while it's still warm, mixing constantly. It doesn't look great at this stage but stick with it! Add the cooked chicken and let it warm through.

To serve, ladle the broth into warmed serving bowls and garnish with the spring onions (scallions), red chilli and a drop or two of sesame oil.

SEARED TUNA WITH GINGER AND SOY DRESSING

Serves 2

Tuna is robust and meaty enough to hold the strong flavours from the fragrant and fruity pink peppercorns. The dressing is delicious on its own and goes so well with any number of fish dishes, especially raw ones. I've borrowed this idea from the great chef and restaurateur Rowley Leigh, and he knows what he's doing!

For the tuna
20g (¾oz) dried pink peppercorns
300g (10½oz) fresh tuna, in
  one piece
2 tbsp olive oil
180g (6oz) baby leaf spinach

For the dressing
75ml (2½fl oz) vegetable oil
2 tbsp light soy sauce
Juice of 1 lemon
1 tsp toasted sesame oil
1 garlic clove, crushed
1 tbsp finely chopped root ginger
2 tbsp finely chopped chives
Salt and freshly ground black
  pepper, to taste

Put the pink peppercorns on a plate and push the tuna down onto them. Turn it over and repeat on the other side, so the tuna is fully covered.

Heat a large frying pan (skillet) almost to smoking point over a high heat, add a splash of olive oil, add the tuna and sear for no more than 1–2 minutes each side. Take the tuna out of the pan and rest on a plate.

Throw the baby leaf spinach into the same pan and sauté until wilted.

For the ginger and soy dressing, put all the ingredients in a bowl and whisk together well.

To serve, put the wilted spinach on a serving dish. Cut the tuna into thick slices, lay them over the spinach and spoon over a generous amount of the dressing before serving.

Serves 2

Pungent fresh horseradish is the perfect foil to rich mackerel. You only get this pungency from a fresh root, so use that rather than a jar of ready-grated stuff for this recipe.

For the vermouth sauce
25g (1oz) unsalted butter
1 banana shallot, finely chopped
Fish stock made with 1 fish stock cube and 300ml (10½fl oz) hot water (alternatively, you can make a fish stock by simmering 250g (9oz) chopped white fish bones from your fishmonger in 300ml (10½fl oz) water for 20 minutes)
125ml (4fl oz) vermouth
2 thyme sprigs
2 white peppercorns
100ml (3½fl oz) double (heavy) cream
Juice of 1 lemon

For the mackerel
100g (3½oz) fresh breadcrumbs
2 tbsp finely grated fresh horseradish
2 medium free-range eggs, beaten
50g (1¾oz) plain (all-purpose) flour
2 mackerel fillets
2 tbsp olive oil
40g (1½oz) butter
Sea salt and freshly ground black pepper

Start by making the vermouth sauce. Heat the butter in a large saucepan. Once melted add the shallot and cook, stirring gently, for 5–10 minutes. Add the fish stock, turn up the heat to high and reduce the liquid to a few concentrated tablespoons (this should take 6–8 minutes). Add the vermouth, thyme and peppercorns and cook until the vermouth is reduced by half, a further 5–10 minutes.

Add the cream and lemon juice and cook for 1–2 minutes more. Strain the sauce through a sieve (strainer) into a clean pan, discarding the contents of the sieve, and season with salt to taste.

For the mackerel, put the breadcrumbs and grated horseradish into a bowl and mix together. Pour the eggs into a second bowl and the plain (all-purpose) flour in a third. Dip the mackerel fillets in the breadcrumb/horseradish mixture first, then into the eggs and, finally, the flour.

Heat the oil and butter in a large frying pan (skillet). When the butter is foaming, add the mackerel fillets and fry the fish on one side for 3 minutes, or until it forms a golden crust. Carefully turn the fillets over and cook the other side for a further 3 minutes.

Serve the cooked mackerel fillets, hot, on a serving plate with the vermouth sauce on the side.

PRAWN ROLLS WITH AVOCADO AND FRESH MANGO SALSA

Serves 4

For the avocado purée
1 ripe avocado, peeled, stoned
    and roughly chopped
1 small green chilli, deseeded
    and finely chopped
Pinch of ground cumin
Juice of 1 lime
2 tbsp olive oil
Sea salt and freshly ground
    black pepper

For the mango salsa
1 ripe mango, peeled
    and chopped
1 tsp chopped fresh
    tarragon leaves
2 spring onions (scallions),
    finely chopped
1 tsp finely chopped root ginger
1 garlic clove, crushed
4 tsp mirin
4 tsp light soy sauce
2 tsp toasted sesame oil

For the prawns
Vegetable oil, for deep-frying
40g (1½oz) plain
    (all-purpose) flour
40g (1½oz) polenta
½ tsp hot smoked paprika
300g (10½oz) raw king prawns
    (jumbo shrimp), peeled
    and deveined

To serve
4 brioche rolls, halved
    and toasted
Handful of rocket (arugula) leaves
1–2 tbsp chilli sauce
1 tbsp mayonnaise

If you're not into prawns (shrimp), you could use strips of chicken cooked in the same way instead, but I think there is something so luxurious about having these flavourful prawns stuffed generously into a soft brioche roll.

To make the avocado purée, put all the ingredients in a food processor and blitz until smooth. Season to taste with salt and pepper.

For the mango salsa, put all the ingredients in a large bowl and stir together. Taste and season.

For the prawns (shrimp), preheat a deep-fat fryer to 180°C (350°F), or half-fill a deep, heavy-based pan with vegetable oil set over a medium-high heat. The oil is hot enough when a small cube of bread dropped into the oil turns golden brown in 40–50 seconds (or you can test the temperature using a probe thermometer).

Mix the flour, polenta and paprika together in a bowl. Dust the prawns in this mixture and shake off the excess. When the oil is hot, carefully add the prawns and deep-fry for 2–3 minutes, or until golden. Remove using a slotted spoon and drain on a plate lined with paper towels.

To serve, spread the bases of the toasted brioche rolls with the avocado purée. Fill the rolls with the fried prawns and rocket (arugula) leaves, followed by the mango salsa. Mix together the mayonnaise and chilli sauce in a small bowl and dollop over before adding the tops of the rolls.

DIM SUM PRAWN DUMPLINGS

Serves 4

For the stock
400ml (14fl oz) chicken stock
Prawn (shrimp) shells (see
    list below)
Ginger and garlic peel (see
    list below)
Chilli trimmings (see list below)
1 garlic clove, peeled and
    smashed but left whole

For the dumplings
250g (9oz) raw shelled prawns
    (shrimp), shells reserved
250g (9oz) pork mince
    (ground pork)
2 garlic cloves, grated,
    peel reserved
1 red chilli, trimmed and chopped,
    trimmings reserved
1 tsp peeled and grated root
    ginger, peel reserved
1 tbsp toasted sesame oil
4 small dried shiitake mushrooms,
    soaked in warm water and
    finely chopped
1 tsp cornflour (cornstarch)
32 ready-made wonton wrappers

To garnish and serve
4 spring onions (scallions),
    trimmed and finely chopped
1 tbsp chopped chives
2 tbsp light soy sauce
1 tbsp Chinese black vinegar
    or rice wine vinegar

These really aren't as complicated to make as you might think. Like all Chinese-style dishes, most of the work is in the initial preparation and collecting all the ingredients together. Once you get the hang of it... easy peasy!

For the stock, put the chicken stock, prawn (shrimp) shells, peelings, trimmings and garlic into a large saucepan and bring to the boil, then turn down the heat and simmer for 30 minutes.

For the prawn dumplings, put all the ingredients (except the wonton wrappers) in a medium food processor and blitz to a smooth paste.

Wet the outside edge of a wonton wrapper with water and put a teaspoon of the filling mixture into the centre. Draw up the sides of the wonton wrapper around the filling, leaving the top exposed. This can be as random as you like. Repeat this process with the remaining wrappers until all the filling has been used up.

Place a large steamer on the hob and cook the dumplings in the steamer for 6–8 minutes (working in batches if needed), or until cooked through.

To serve, strain the stock into four warmed bowls (discard the flavourings). Add the dumplings and garnish with the spring onions (scallions) and chives and drizzle over the soy sauce and vinegar. Serve immediately while nice and hot.

Friday Night

MALFATTI WITH TUNA

Serves 4

Malfatti, from the Lombardy region of northern Italy, are misshapen dumplings ('malfatti' means 'badly made'). They are much lighter than ordinary gnocchi and more interesting. There's no need to be a perfectionist about this – the more rustic they look, the more authentic they become. It's best to drain the ricotta the night before so that it dries out a little – this will help the mix bind together.

I've served this with griddled fresh tuna, pesto and a great tomato sauce, but if you're pressed for time, a simple sage butter would make for a delicious quick-fix supper.

For the tomato sauce
2 tbsp olive oil
2 shallots, finely chopped
1 garlic clove, finely chopped
2 tsp balsamic vinegar
400g (14oz) tin good-quality
    plum tomatoes
Stalks from 1 bunch of basil
    (pick the leaves for the
    pesto, below)

For the pesto
Leaves from 1 bunch of basil (set
    aside a few leaves to serve)
2 garlic cloves, finely chopped
75g (2½oz) toasted pine nuts, plus
    extra to serve
100g (3½oz) Parmesan, grated
Extra virgin olive oil, for drizzling

For the malfatti
500g (1lb 2oz) spinach
50g (1¾oz) semolina flour
50g (1¾oz) '00' flour
250g (9oz) ricotta, drained
    overnight in muslin
    (cheesecloth)
1 medium free-range egg, beaten
150g (5½oz) Parmesan, grated
¼ nutmeg, freshly grated
Sea salt and freshly ground
    black pepper

To serve
400g (14oz) fresh tuna
Basil leaves

For the tomato sauce, heat a medium sauté pan over a medium-high heat and add the oil. Once hot, add the shallots and garlic, then cook, stirring, for 2–3 minutes, or until the shallots are soft. Add the balsamic vinegar.

Now throw in the tomatoes and the basil stalks and cook, stirring occasionally, for a further 10 minutes, or until the sauce thickens. Cool a little, then transfer to a food processor and blend to a purée.

For the pesto, put all the ingredients except the extra virgin olive oil into a pestle and mortar (or into the cleaned food processer) and blend to a paste. Gradually add the extra virgin olive oil until you have the pesto consistency you like.

For the malfatti, boil or steam the spinach for 3 minutes until tender. Drain in a colander or sieve (strainer) and drain any excess water from the spinach, using your hands to squeeze out as much liquid as possible. Once cool enough to handle, roughly chop the spinach.

Combine the two types of flour and the ricotta in a large bowl and mix until it looks like moist breadcrumbs. Stir in the egg and grated Parmesan. Add a good pinch of sea salt and black pepper, the nutmeg and the chopped spinach and stir to combine.

Roll into 12–16 even balls about the size of a large walnut and set aside on a baking tray.

Bring a large pan of salted water to the boil. Carefully add the malfatti, bring the water back to the boil, then simmer over a gentle heat, so as not to break them up, for 2–3 minutes, or until the malfatti float to the surface of the water, just as gnocchi do. Remove the cooked malfatti with a slotted spoon and drain on a baking tray lined with paper towels and keep warm.

To serve, heat a large ridged griddle pan over a high heat. Season the tuna with sea salt and black pepper and cook on the hot griddle pan for 1–2 minutes on each side, depending on how you like your tuna cooked. Allow to rest for 3 minutes.

Spoon the warmed tomato sauce and the pesto onto each serving plate. Top with the hot malfatti and slice (or tear) over the tuna. Scatter over the reserved basil leaves and toasted pine nuts.

CUMIN-ROASTED CAULIFLOWER WITH SICHUAN PEPPER AND PEANUT DIP

Serves 2

Packed full of flavours, this vegetarian dish is a real winner, even for hardened carnivores like me. I love the numbing effect of the Sichuan peppercorns but if they aren't your thing, then you can just leave them out. There are so many other flavours involved, the dish won't be poorer for it.

For the cauliflower
2 tbsp grapeseed or vegetable oil
1 tbsp cumin seeds
1 whole medium cauliflower, separated into florets, leaves kept and trimmed

For the dip
2 tsp Sichuan peppercorns, crushed in a pestle and mortar
1 red chilli, chopped
1 tbsp finely chopped root ginger
2 garlic cloves, finely chopped
2 tbsp sesame seeds
3 tbsp vegetable oil
1 tbsp chilli oil
1 tbsp soy sauce
2 tsp toasted sesame oil
5 tbsp crunchy peanut butter

For the topping
25g (1oz) cashews or peanuts, toasted in a dry pan and finely chopped
½ garlic clove, finely chopped
25g (1oz) breadcrumbs, toasted in a dry pan
¼ tbsp black sesame seeds

To garnish
15g (½oz) bunch of Thai basil, leaves picked
4 spring onions (scallions), finely chopped

Preheat the oven to 220°C/200°C fan/425°F/gas mark 7. Mix the oil and cumin seeds together in a bowl.

Put the cauliflower on a baking tray and pour the cumin oil over the top of the florets. Roast the cauliflower in the oven for 20–30 minutes until soft. For the last 5 minutes of cooking, add the cauliflower leaves to the baking tray and roast those too.

To make the dip, put the Sichuan peppercorns, chilli, ginger, garlic and sesame seeds in a heatproof bowl.

Heat the vegetable and chilli oil in a small pan. When hot, pour the oil over the Sichuan peppercorn mixture. It should crackle and pop. Add the soy sauce and sesame oil and whisk in the peanut butter. You might need to loosen the dip with a little water to give it more of a dressing consistency.

For the topping, mix all the ingredients together, either chopping by hand or using a food processor, to a fine crumb and set aside.

To serve, spoon a generous pool of peanut dressing onto each plate and top with the roasted cauliflower. Garnish with the peanut and breadcrumb topping and, lastly, the Thai basil leaves and spring onions (scallions).

Friday Night

SPICY CRISP-FRIED CAULIFLOWER

**Serves 4
as a starter
or snack**

For the cauliflower
Vegetable oil, for deep-frying
1 large cauliflower, broken
    into florets
4 tbsp chickpea flour
5 tbsp cornflour (cornstarch)
1 tbsp chilli paste
6 fresh curry leaves,
    finely chopped
½ tbsp garam masala
Sea salt and freshly ground
    black pepper

For the cucumber and yoghurt
½ tsp ground cumin
½ tsp black mustard seeds
1 green chilli, chopped
2 tbsp cashews, chopped
1 cucumber, grated
155g (5½oz) full-fat Greek yoghurt

To garnish
8 fresh curry leaves
2 red chillies, sliced

This is inspired by the famous Goan street food Gobi 65. The cauliflower pieces fried in this spicy batter, served with the cooling aromatic cucumber and yoghurt, make the perfect starter or light snack.

To cook the cauliflower, use a deep-fat fryer set at 180°C (350°F), or half-fill a deep, heavy-based saucepan with oil set over a medium-high heat. The oil is hot enough when a small cube of bread dropped into the oil turns golden brown in 40–50 seconds (or you can test the temperature using a probe thermometer).

Bring a saucepan of salted water to the boil, then plunge the cauliflower florets into the boiling water for 2 minutes. Drain and refresh in cold water. Set aside.

In a large bowl, make a smooth batter by mixing together the chickpea flour and cornflour (cornstarch), the chilli paste, chopped curry leaves and garam masala. Gradually add just enough cold water to form a batter with the consistency of single (light) cream.

Lightly coat the blanched cauliflower florets in the batter, shake off the excess and deep-fry in the hot oil for 2 minutes until golden brown. Remove using a slotted spoon, drain on a plate lined with paper towels and keep warm. Leave the fryer on for the garnish.

For the cucumber and yoghurt, toast the cumin, mustard seeds, green chilli and cashews for 2 minutes in a dry pan over a medium heat.

Put the grated cucumber in a clean dish towel and squeeze out as much excess water as you can. Throw it into a bowl with the yoghurt and add the roasted spice mix. Stir and season with salt and pepper.

Arrange the fried cauliflower in a serving bowl. Deep-fry the curry leaves and sliced green chillies and scatter over the cauliflower. Serve the cucumber and yoghurt alongside.

ROSEMARY CHICKEN WITH MISO MUSHROOMS AND GARLIC MAYONNAISE

Serves 4

The addition of the miso mushrooms ups the ante on the umami front, and the garlic mayonnaise is there for added delicious naughtiness.

For the chicken
1 small (1.3–1.5kg/3lb–3lb 5oz) free-range chicken
50g (1¾oz) butter, softened
4 rosemary sprigs, leaves chopped
2 banana shallots, quartered
1 bay leaf
1 garlic bulb, broken into cloves, skin on
Sea salt and freshly ground black pepper
1 x 100g (3½oz) bag of watercress, to serve

For the miso mushrooms
2 tbsp olive oil
4 large field mushrooms, cleaned but left whole
2 tbsp soy sauce
2 tsp white miso

For the garlic mayonnaise
6 tbsp mayonnaise
3 tbsp chicken fat and juices from the roasted chicken
4 roasted garlic cloves, from the roasted chicken

Preheat the oven to 200°C/180°C fan/400°F/gas mark 6. Smear the chicken all over with the butter, sprinkle half the chopped rosemary over the bird and stuff the reminder inside the cavity. Season well with salt and pepper. Throw the shallots, bay leaf and garlic cloves into a roasting tin and stick the chicken on top. Add a teacup (250ml/9fl oz) or so) of water to the tin.

Roast for about 1 hour, or until the juices run clear when pierced with a skewer in the thickest part of the thigh. Leave to rest for 15 minutes then pour off the juices and set aside to use later.

Meanwhile, for the miso mushrooms, heat the oil in a pan over a medium heat, add the mushrooms and brown, stirring occasionally, for 5 minutes. In a bowl, whisk together the soy sauce, miso and 4 tablespoons of water. Add this mixture to the pan, turn down the heat to low, then simmer for 10 minutes, or until the mushrooms have softened up.

To make the garlic mayonnaise, squeeze out the soft garlic flesh from the 4 roasted cloves into a small bowl. Stir in the mayo, chicken fat and pan juices.

Serve the chicken on a warmed serving plate with the watercress and miso mushrooms, with the garlic mayonnaise alongside.

BUTTERMILK FRIED CHICKEN AND CHARRED PINEAPPLE SALSA

Serves 4–6

Buttermilk has a tenderizing effect on meat, much like yoghurt, so don't leave the chicken in the marinade too long or it'll start to break down. It's quite widely available these days but if you struggle to find it, then a full-fat Greek yoghurt will work.

There are a million recipes for fried chicken out there, but this is the one I usually come back to. Adjust the spices to your taste, but a little heat works beautifully with the cooling salsa and sour cream.

For the chicken

12 boneless, skinless chicken
    thighs, cut in half lengthways
200ml (7fl oz) buttermilk
1 medium free-range egg, beaten
2 tbsp Dijon mustard
1 tsp sea salt
1 tsp freshly ground black pepper
Vegetable oil, for deep-frying

For the spiced flour

200g (7oz) plain (all-purpose) flour
4 tsp sweet (not hot)
    smoked paprika
2 tsp baking powder
2 tsp cayenne pepper
2 tsp garlic salt
1 tsp sea salt
1 tsp freshly ground black pepper

For the pineapple salsa

1 small pineapple, core removed,
    cut lengthways into thick strips
1 red onion, sliced
½ tsp salt
Juice of 1 lime
2 jalapeño chilies, deseeded
    and sliced
1 bunch of basil

To serve

200ml (7fl oz) sour cream
1 tbsp hot sauce of your choice
1 lime, cut into wedges

Start by marinating the chicken. Put the thighs in a shallow bowl with the buttermilk, egg and Dijon mustard, then season with the salt and pepper. Leave to marinate for an hour, covered in the fridge.

Meanwhile, mix together all the ingredients for the spiced flour in a shallow bowl and set aside.

To make the pineapple salsa, heat a ridged griddle pan (or a barbecue) to a high heat. Place the pineapple strips on the griddle and cook on both sides for 3–4 minutes until charred and soft. Remove and allow to cool, collecting any juices from the pan in a bowl.

Put the onion, salt and lime juice in a bowl and leave for 5–10 minutes until the onion has softened. Add the jalapeños and about six grinds of black pepper from a pepper mill. Chop the pineapple into 1cm (½in) pieces and tip them and all the juices from the pan into the bowl. Tear in the basil leaves and stir through at the last minute.

To finish the chicken, heat a deep-fat fryer to 180°C (350°F), or half-fill a deep, heavy-based pan with oil set over a medium-high heat. The oil is hot enough when a small cube of bread dropped into the oil turns golden brown in 40–50 seconds (or you can test the temperature using a probe thermometer).

Lift each piece of chicken from the marinade and shake off any excess liquid. Dip the chicken thighs in the spiced flour and press gently to coat evenly. Working in batches, use tongs to carefully place the chicken thighs into the fryer and cook for 6–8 minutes until golden. Remove with a slotted spoon and drain on a plate lined with paper towels. Keep each batch warm while you cook the rest.

Make sure the chicken is cooked through by cutting a piece in half and checking that the centre is white, not pink. If needed, cook for a further 5 minutes in the oven at 200°C/180°C fan/400°F/gas mark 6.

Serve immediately with a bowl of the pineapple salsa, a good splodge of sour cream and hot sauce on top, and the lime wedges for squeezing over.

PORK BANH MI WITH CRISPY BITS AND CARROT PICKLE

Serves 2

I know it looks like a lot of ingredients, but these Vietnamese-inspired burgers are simply delicious, and well worth the effort. All the herby, sweet, spicy, sour and savoury elements make it a real taste sensation.

For the crispy bits
Vegetable oil, for frying
1 banana shallot, thinly sliced
2 red chillies, thinly sliced
2 garlic cloves, thinly sliced
100g (3½oz) cornflour (cornstarch)
Sea salt and freshly ground
    black pepper

For the carrot pickle
2 carrots, very thinly peeled
2 tbsp rice wine vinegar
1 lemongrass stick, soft inner part
    only, finely chopped
1 tbsp palm sugar
Zest and juice of 1 lime

For the sriracha and herb mayonnaise
1 tsp sriracha chilli sauce
4 tbsp mayonnaise
1 tbsp chopped Thai basil
1 tbsp chopped coriander (cilantro)
1 tbsp chopped mint

For the burgers
400g (14oz) pork mince (ground pork)
2 red chillies, deseeded and
    finely chopped
2 garlic cloves, crushed
2cm (¾in) piece root ginger,
    finely chopped
2 tbsp finely chopped coriander
3 tbsp fish sauce
2 tbsp vegetable oil

To serve
1 small baguette, halved straight
    down the middle
½ baby gem lettuce, leaves separated
4 cucumber slices

Start by making the crispy bits: heat a 2cm (¾in) layer of vegetable oil in a heavy-based pan over a high heat.

Mix the shallot, chilli and garlic in a bowl and sprinkle them with the cornflour (cornstarch), shaking off the excess. When the oil is hot enough to brown a small cube of bread in 40–50 seconds, add the shallot, chilli and garlic to the hot oil and cook for 3–5 minutes, or until crisp and golden brown. Remove using a slotted spoon and drain on a plate lined with paper towels. Season with salt and pepper straight away.

To make the carrot pickle, mix the carrots, vinegar, lemongrass, palm sugar, lime zest and juice together in a bowl and set aside.

Mix the sriracha, mayonnaise and all the herbs together in a separate bowl and set aside.

For the pork burgers, throw together the pork, chilli, garlic, ginger, coriander (cilantro) and fish sauce in a bowl and mix well. Season with salt and pepper. Form into golf ball-sized balls then flatten slightly.

Heat the oil in a frying pan (skillet). When hot, gently fry the pork balls all over for 3–4 minutes until cooked through (cut one open to check there is no remaining pink in the meat).

To serve, pile up the sliced baguettes with the pork balls, all the toppings, the carrot pickle, mayo and crispy bits. Dive in!

Friday Night

SPICED LAMB FLATBREAD

Serves 8 as
a snack

For the flatbreads
240g (8½oz) strong white
    flour (bread flour), plus
    extra for dusting
7g (2¼ tsp) sachet
    fast-action yeast
1 tsp fine salt
2 tbsp olive oil
150ml (5fl oz) warm water

For the lamb topping
500g (1lb 2oz) lamb mince
    (ground lamb)
1 tsp ground cumin
1 tsp ground coriander
1 tbsp dried thyme
1 tbsp dried oregano
1 red chilli, deseeded and
    finely chopped
2 garlic cloves, finely chopped
2 large tomatoes, skin removed
    and finely grated
Sea salt and freshly ground
    black pepper

For the herbed yoghurt
150g (5½oz) full-fat Greek yoghurt
1 garlic clove, finely chopped
½ green chilli, deseeded and
    finely chopped
1 tbsp chopped fresh mint

To serve
25g (1oz) flatleaf parsley,
    leaves picked
100g (3½oz) feta cheese,
    crumbled
100g (3½oz) walnuts, toasted
    and roughly chopped
1 red onion, finely chopped
4 pickled chillies, 2 red and
    2 green, roughly chopped
Juice of 1 lemon

Turkish and Cypriot-inspired lamb flatbreads, packed full
of big punchy flavours.

To make the flatbreads, mix the flour, yeast and salt in a large
bowl. Make a well in the centre and gradually add the olive oil
and warm water and mix to form a dough.

Dust the work surface with flour and knead the dough for
5 minutes, or until smooth.

Divide the dough into four equal pieces and roll each
piece into a ball. Transfer to a baking tray lined with baking
paper, cover with a clean cloth and leave to prove for 1 hour.

Meanwhile, for the spiced lamb topping, stir all the
ingredients together in a bowl and season with salt
and pepper.

Next, mix the yoghurt, garlic, chilli and mint together in
a small bowl. Taste and season, then set aside.

Preheat the oven to 240°C/220°C fan/475°F/gas mark
8 and place a heavy baking tray (if you have a pizza stone
use it here) inside the oven to heat.

On a lightly floured surface, roll each ball of dough out
into long oval shapes about 5mm (¼in) thick.

Spread the spiced lamb mixture evenly on each flatbread.
Bake on the preheated baking tray (or pizza stone) for 8–10
minutes. Check that the base is crispy and the meat is
cooked through.

To serve, sprinkle over the parsley leaves, crumbled feta,
walnuts, red onion and chopped pickled chillies. Squeeze
the lemon juice over and serve with the yoghurt dip,
spooning some over the top if you like.

CAPE MALAY LAMB CURRY WITH HERB COUSCOUS

Serves 4

Cape Malay food originates from South Africa, where the coming together of people from Indonesia and India gave rise to a particular style of sweet and fruity curry. Dried fruit is often used. Here I've used dried apricots and coconut. Another great example of Cape Malay cooking is bobotie, a national dish of South Africa. Bobotie is a sweet, spicy beef dish with a savoury custard topping (not too far removed from a moussaka). I can assure you both dishes are totally delicious.

1 boneless shoulder of lamb,
    diced into 2.5cm (1in) cubes

For the lamb marinade
4 tbsp vegetable oil
1 tsp ground coriander
1 tsp ground cumin
1 tsp garam masala
1 tsp ground turmeric
1 tbsp tamarind paste
2 small dried chillies
1 tsp fennel seeds
1 cinnamon stick, about 8cm (3in)
4 garlic cloves, grated
1 red chilli, finely chopped
1cm (½in) piece root ginger,
    finely grated

For the curry
2 tbsp sunflower oil
2 onions, thinly sliced
2 garlic cloves, sliced
2cm (¾in) piece root ginger,
    finely grated
2 tsp dried chilli flakes
1 tsp fennel seeds
2 tbsp tomato purée
    (tomato paste)
400g (14oz) tin chopped tomatoes
250–300ml (9–10½fl oz)
    lamb stock
125g (4½oz) dried apricots,
    roughly chopped
2 tbsp apricot chutney
75g (2½oz) desiccated coconut
Sea salt and freshly ground
    black pepper

Start by marinating the lamb: put all the ingredients in a bowl and mix well. Add the lamb, cover and leave to marinate in the fridge for a few hours.

Bring the meat to room temperature before you make a start on the curry. Heat a large sauté pan over a high heat and add the oil. Once hot, add the onions, garlic and ginger and cook, stirring, for 5 minutes, or until the onions are soft. Add the chilli flakes and fennel seeds and cook for a further 1 minute.

Stir in the tomato purée (tomato paste) and tinned tomatoes then add the marinated lamb. Pour in the lamb stock, cover with the lid, reduce the heat to low and simmer for 1–1½ hours.

About 10 minutes from the end of the cooking time, add the dried apricots, apricot chutney and desiccated coconut and simmer, stirring. Season with salt and pepper.

To make the couscous, mix all the ingredients in a large bowl and season.

Serve the curry with the couscous, garnished with the coriander (cilantro) and grated fresh coconut.

For the herb couscous
500g (1lb 2oz) cooked couscous
¼ cucumber, diced
Seeds from 1 pomegranate
¼ bunch of basil, finely chopped
¼ bunch of flatleaf parsley,
    finely chopped
¼ bunch of coriander (cilantro),
    finely chopped
100g (3½oz) dried apricots,
    finely chopped
4 spring onions (scallions),
    finely chopped

To serve
½ bunch of fresh coriander,
    roughly chopped
50g (1¾oz) fresh coconut, grated

DURBAN BUNNY CHOW WITH PRAWNS

Serves 4

Don't let the name fool you, this is a fantastic dish, and possibly the best way to eat a curry. Bunny chow is a traditional South African curry that is served in a hollowed-out loaf of bread. It's a speciality of the east coast city of Durban, which is home to a large Indian population and, with it, a big emphasis on curries and spices. There's a lot of speculation about why this curry is served in a loaf of bread but, whatever reason, the result is genius.

I've used king prawns (jumbo shrimp) here, but a more traditional filling would use lamb or mutton.

2 tbsp vegetable oil
2 tsp black mustard seeds
1 onion, thinly sliced
3 garlic cloves, grated
1 heaped tbsp grated root ginger
1 green chilli, finely chopped
16 fresh curry leaves (or 20 dried)
2 tsp ground cumin
1 whole star anise
1 cinnamon stick
2 tsp ground coriander
1 tsp ground turmeric
2 tsp tomato purée (tomato paste)
4 plum tomatoes, deseeded and finely chopped
100g (3½oz) tamarind paste
20 raw king prawns (jumbo shrimp), peeled and deveined
Sea salt and freshly ground black pepper

To serve
2 small unsliced whole white loaves, lids cut off and with the middle removed (save for breadcrumbs)
2 tbsp coconut flakes, toasted in a dry pan
2 tbsp curry leaves (fresh or dried), fried in a small pan of hot oil

Heat the oil in a large pan over a medium heat. When hot, add the mustard seeds and let them pop for a minute or two. Add the onion, garlic, ginger and chilli and fry, stirring, until soft. Add the curry leaves and other spices and cook, stirring, for 2 minutes more.

Add the tomato purée (tomato paste), chopped tomatoes, tamarind paste and the prawns (shrimp), then pour in enough water to cover. Simmer for 10 minutes, or until the prawns are pink and cooked through. Taste and season with sea salt and black pepper. Remove the star anise and cinnamon stick before serving.

Spoon the curry into the hollowed-out loaves and garnish with the toasted coconut flakes and fried curry leaves before serving.

DUCK MASSAMAN CURRY

Serves 4

This rich southern Thai curry is a fusion between Thai, Indian and Malay influences. Its characteristic spices, including cinnamon, nutmeg and cloves, were originally brought to Thailand by Muslim traders.

Any leftover curry paste can kept covered and stored in the fridge for up to 2 months.

For the curry paste
2 garlic cloves, chopped
1 red chilli, chopped
1 tsp Thai fermented
    shrimp paste
30g (1oz) toasted peanuts, chopped
1 banana shallot, chopped
1 thumb-sized piece root
    ginger, chopped
2 lemongrass sticks, outer skin
    removed and core chopped
2 tsp tamarind paste
Pinch of ground mace
Pinch of freshly grated nutmeg
Pinch of ground cinnamon
2 tsp palm sugar
2 tbsp fish sauce
1 tsp ground coriander
1 tsp ground cumin
2 whole cloves

For the duck curry
2 duck breasts, skin removed and
    skin frozen for at least 40 minutes,
    meat chopped into 1cm (½ in) dice
2 tbsp vegetable oil
1 onion, chopped
2 bay leaves
3 cardamom pods
1 large potato, diced
3 tbsp curry paste (from the
    recipe above)
1 tbsp palm sugar
400ml (14fl oz) coconut milk
Sea salt and freshly ground
    black pepper

To serve
2 tbsp chopped coriander (cilantro)
50g (1¾oz) roasted peanuts,
    roughly chopped
Steamed jasmine rice (cook
    60–70g (2¼–2½oz per person)

Put all the ingredients for the curry paste into a food processor and blend to a fairly smooth paste.

Remove the duck skin from the freezer and cut very thinly using a sharp knife. Heat a small pan over a high heat. When hot, add the duck skin and cook, stirring, until crispy. Season with salt and pepper and set aside.

For the duck curry, heat a medium sauté pan over a medium heat, then add the oil. Once hot, add the onion and the spices and cook, stirring, until soft – this should take about 10 minutes. Add the potatoes, curry paste and palm sugar.

Stir in the coconut milk and simmer it gently over a low heat until the potatoes are just tender when tested with the tip of a sharp knife, about 10 minutes.

Add the duck meat and continue to simmer for 5–6 more minutes over a low heat. Don't let it boil or the meat will become tough. Taste and season with salt and pepper.

Spoon the curry into serving bowls and garnish with the chopped coriander (cilantro) and peanuts, then top with the crispy duck skin. Serve with steamed jasmine rice.

Serves 2

There's a bit of a mad mix of food cultures going on here, but this tostada tastes fantastic. It's my take on the ubiquitous crispy beef dish you get from the Chinese takeaway, but my version contains way more beef!

Marinate the beef for this dish the day before you want to serve it. Serve these tostadas with the Jalapeño Relish on page 118.

For the crispy beef
2 x 200g (7oz) sirloin steaks, fat removed, cut into thin strips
2 tbsp vegetable oil
2 tsp mirin

For the marinade
1 tbsp finely chopped root ginger
2 garlic cloves, finely chopped
1 tbsp mirin or 1 tbsp brown sugar
1 tbsp cornflour (cornstarch)
3 tbsp soy sauce
1 medium free-range egg, beaten

For the sauce
1 garlic clove, finely chopped
1 tsp grated root ginger
100ml (3½fl oz) light soy sauce
100ml (3½fl oz) mirin
100ml (3½fl oz) water
2 tsp soft light brown sugar
Juice of ½ lemon
½ tsp cornflour (cornstarch)

For the seasoned flour
1 tbsp white sesame seeds
1 tsp whole black peppercorns, crushed in a mortar and pestle
1 tsp Sichuan peppercorns, crushed in a mortar and pestle
2 tbsp cornflour (cornstarch)
4 tbsp plain (all-purpose) flour

To serve
4 tbsp crème fraîche
4 soft flour tortillas, warmed
25g (1oz) rocket (arugula) leaves
Jalapeño Relish (see page 118)
Small handful of coriander (cilantro) leaves

Mix all the marinade ingredients together in a bowl or shallow dish. Add the sliced beef, mix well, cover and leave to marinate in the fridge for 24 hours. Bring to room temperature for 20 minutes before cooking.

To make the sauce, put the garlic, ginger, soy sauce, mirin, water, sugar and lemon juice in a small saucepan, then whisk in the cornflour (cornstarch). Bring to a gentle simmer over a low heat and cook, stirring, until reduced by half, about 5 minutes. Set aside.

Preheat the oven to 170°C/150°C fan/325°F/gas mark 3.

Combine all the seasoned flour ingredients in a bowl and mix well.

Heat a wok over a high heat. When hot, add the 2 tbsp vegetable oil. Remove the beef strips from the marinade, splash with the 2 tsp mirin and dip into the seasoned flour. Shake off the excess, and drop the beef strips into the hot oil. Fry, stirring until crisp, in small batches for around 2 minutes for each batch. Remove with a slotted spoon and keep warm on a baking tray in the oven while you cook the remaining batches.

To serve, spoon 1 tablespoon of crème fraîche onto the base of each warmed tortilla, add a few rocket (arugula) leaves and divide the crispy beef evenly between the tortillas. Drizzle over some of the sauce and spoon over the Jalapeño Relish. Scatter over the coriander (cilantro) leaves and serve immediately.

Friday Night

ALPINE-STYLE STUFFED BREAD

Serves 2

I love skiing and try to get to the mountains every year, mainly because it's the greatest feeling to come in out of the snow and eat delicious mountain cheese, fantastic local salami and homemade bread around a chalet fire.

I was served this bread in the most beautiful surroundings of the French Alps. The sun was shining over the mountains and I had in front of me the biggest stuffed-cheese, meaty treat you've ever seen. It was a moment to savour.

For the bread dough
250g (9oz) strong white flour (bread flour), plus extra for kneading and rolling out
7g (2¼ tsp) sachet fast-action yeast
1 tsp fine salt
150–200ml (5–7fl oz) warm water

For the filling
2 tbsp olive oil
¼ savoy cabbage, cored, sliced, blanched and refreshed under cold water
2 x 140g (5oz) herb sausages, cooked and each sliced into 8 pieces
130g (4½oz) smoked sausage, cooked and cut into 8 pieces
200g (7oz) new potatoes, boiled and thinly sliced
100ml (3½fl oz) crème fraîche
150g (5½oz) Gruyère or Reblochon cheese, grated
Sea salt and freshly ground black pepper

To make the bread dough, put the flour in a large mixing bowl, add the yeast and salt and mix by hand (or you can mix it in the bowl of a stand mixer, if you have one).

Gradually add the water a bit at a time and mix until it just comes together as a dough (you may not need all the water). Flour a work surface, then knead the dough by hand (or knead in the mixer using the dough hook attachment) for about 5 minutes until you have a smooth dough. Transfer the dough to a lightly floured bowl, cover and leave to rise until it has doubled in size, about 1 hour.

Preheat the oven 240°C/220°C fan/475°F/gas mark 8. Line a baking tray with baking paper.

To make the filling, heat a medium frying pan (skillet) over a medium heat and add the olive oil. Once hot, add the blanched cabbage and fry for 2–3 minutes, or until wilted.

Transfer the cabbage to a bowl, add the sliced sausages and new potatoes, then gently mix in the crème fraîche and cheese. Season with salt and pepper and mix to combine.

Once the dough has doubled in size, knead it gently to knock out any large pockets of air.

Dust a work surface with flour and roll out the dough to a 30cm (12in) circle. Place the filling on one half of the rolled-out dough circle then fold the other half over to make a semicircle, a bit like a calzone pizza. Seal and crimp the edges and transfer to the lined baking tray.

Bake in the oven for 20 minutes, or until the crust is golden brown. When you tap the bottom and it sounds hollow, it is cooked.

Transfer the bread onto a wooden board for serving, then slice and share.

We seem to have staggered breakfasts in our house. I'm an early bird and usually start the day with a kitchen workout, mooching about, whipping up something simple but delicious to set me up for the day ahead – maybe a healthy juice, some Greek yoghurt and granola or a spicy egg-based dish that kicks the taste buds into action. Whatever it is, it's always accompanied by several strong espressos.

The later risers will generally head straight into brunch; kitchen mayhem generally ensues and fights over who is going to empty the dishwasher abound. I try to drown out all the chaos with some upbeat weekend radio vibes, and treat myself to homemade biscuits or some other sweet treat before I start thinking about what to cook for supper.

These breakfast, brunch and snack ideas will enliven your weekend mornings and distract you from hangovers, rowdy children and the other dangers of family life. Cook up a few eggs, read the weekend papers and relax.

Breakfast and Brunch

BLACKBERRY, RICOTTA AND CITRUS PANCAKES

Serves 4

A classic breakfast staple that's very simple to knock together. The addition of the ricotta gives these pancakes a deliciously smooth interior. You can choose whatever soft fruit you fancy, but the combination of blackberries and blackberry liqueur or cassis gives these a luxurious feel.

You will need to strain the ricotta the evening before you want to make these pancakes – line a colander with muslin (cheesecloth), place over a large bowl and add the ricotta. Leave it to strain overnight in the fridge.

250g (9oz) blackberries
5 tbsp blackberry liqueur (crème de mûre) or crème de cassis
3 medium free-range eggs, separated
250g (9oz) ricotta, strained overnight
50g (1¾oz) golden caster (superfine) sugar
½ tsp vanilla extract
Zest of 1 orange
Zest of 1 lemon
50g (1¾oz) plain (all-purpose) flour
15g (½oz) butter
2 tbsp vegetable oil

To serve
2 tbsp icing (confectioners') sugar
2 tbsp chopped blanched hazelnuts
4 tbsp full-fat Greek yoghurt
4 tbsp maple syrup

Put the blackberries and blackberry liqueur or crème de cassis in a bowl and leave to macerate for at least 15 minutes.

Meanwhile, mix the 3 egg yolks with 1 of the egg whites in a separate bowl. Add the strained ricotta, sugar, vanilla and the orange and lemon zests, then gently mix in the flour.

Whisk the two remaining egg whites in a mixing bowl until they form stiff peaks. Gently fold in half the macerated blackberries (set the rest aside) and the egg yolk and ricotta mixture to form a batter with the consistency of thick whipped cream.

To make the pancakes, melt the butter in a large frying pan (skillet), then add the oil. When the butter is foaming. drop the batter in tablespoonfuls into the hot pan, making sure you leave enough space for them to spread. The batter makes enough for 8–10 pancakes.

Fry for 2–3 minutes on each side in the oil and butter, using a spatula to turn them, until golden in colour on both sides. Repeat until the remaining batter is used up, keeping the cooked pancakes warm until you are ready to serve.

Serve the pancakes dusted with the icing (confectioners') sugar and garnish with the chopped hazelnuts, yoghurt, maple syrup and the remaining macerated blackberries.

APRICOT AND ALMOND PASTRY SWIRLS

Makes 8

Plain (all-purpose) flour,
    for dusting
1 x 320g (11oz) packet all-butter
    puff pastry
1 x 400g (14oz) jar best-quality
    apricot jam (jelly)
100g (3½oz) whole blanched
    almonds, chopped
85g (3oz) dried apricots, soaked
    in boiling water for 20 minutes
    to plump up
1 medium free-range egg, beaten
25g (1oz) toasted flaked almonds,
    crushed in your hands, to serve

A simple but rewarding breakfast snack. You can swap in any flavoured jam (jelly) you fancy. As long as you have a packet of puff pastry in your fridge or freezer, you have a rather impressive breakfast option at your fingertips.

Preheat the oven to 210°C/190°C fan/415°F/gas mark 6–7. Line a 40cm x 27cm (16in x 10¾in) baking tray with baking paper.

Lightly dust a work surface with flour and roll out the puff pastry to a rectangle roughly 30cm x 50cm (12in x 20in), and 3mm (⅛in) thick. Spread 350g (12oz) of the apricot jam (jelly) over the pastry, reserving the remaining jam for the glaze later. Sprinkle over the chopped almonds. Drain the soaked apricots, roughly chop them and scatter them over the almonds.

Starting from the long edge closest to you, roll the topped pastry into a long sausage shape. Trim the two ends to straighten them, then cut the roll into 8 equal slices. Place the pastry slices of side by side in a ring shape on the lined baking tray. Using a pastry brush, brush the top with the beaten egg.

Bake the swirls in the preheated oven for 30–35 minutes, or until cooked through (gently pull them apart and check the inside). You might need to place a piece of foil over the top to prevent them from burning if they're browning too quickly.

Put the remaining apricot jam in a small saucepan, add 1 tablespoon of water, then warm through over a low heat.

Brush the still-warm pastry swirls with the reserved apricot jam glaze and scatter over the crushed toasted flaked almonds. Allow to stand for 30 minutes before pulling apart and serving with a nice cup of tea.

GREEK YOGHURT WITH BLUEBERRIES, GRANOLA AND ALMOND BUTTER

Serves 4

The combination of freshness, acidity and crunch is great, but you could swap in any ripe, seasonal fruit that takes your fancy. The granola is also easily adapted to whatever nuts and seeds you have to hand, but I particularly like the sesame seeds in this one.

This makes more than you will need for 4 servings, so store what's left over in an airtight container for up to 2 months.

500g (1lb 2oz) full-fat
   Greek yoghurt

For the granola
100g (3½oz) pecans
100g (3½oz) almonds
50g (1¾oz) pine nuts
50g (1¾oz) sesame seeds
50g (1¾oz) desiccated
   (shredded) coconut
200g (7oz) raisins, soaked in
   boiling water for 10 minutes
   to soften
200g (7oz) jumbo rolled oats
½ tsp ground ginger
1 tsp ground cinnamon
1 tsp flaked sea salt
5 tbsp maple syrup
4 tbsp vegetable or coconut oil

To serve
150g (5½oz) blueberries
4 tbsp almond butter, loosened
   with 1 tbsp water

Preheat the oven to 200°C/180°C fan/400°F/gas mark 6.

Put the nuts, seeds, desiccated (shredded) coconut, raisins, oats and spices in a large deep baking tray and season with the sea salt.

Warm the maple syrup and the oil in a small pan over a medium heat, then pour it over the ingredients in the baking tray. Mix well to combine.

Transfer to the oven and bake for 20–30 minutes until golden. Shuffle the granola around in the baking tray from time to time to move the browned edges to the middle and vice versa so the finished granola will have an evenly golden finished colour. Set aside to cool.

To serve, spoon the yoghurt into serving bowls, scatter over the granola, top with the blueberries and dollop over the almond butter.

Makes 8–10
slices

370g (13oz) plain
(all-purpose) flour
3 tbsp baking powder
1–2 tsp salt
160g (5¾oz) caster
(superfine) sugar
80g (2¾oz) desiccated
(shredded) coconut
300ml (10½fl oz) coconut milk
2 large free-range eggs, beaten
1 tsp vanilla extract
75g (2½oz) butter, melted and
kept warm

For the raspberry cream
100g (3½oz) crème fraîche
100g (3½oz) mascarpone
1–2 tsp good-quality raspberry
jam (jelly)
150g raspberries, to serve

This is more cake than bread, I'd say. It's especially delicious toasted in a dry pan to crisp the edges a little. This works well as a stand-alone brunch treat or as a sweet snack at any time of the day.

Preheat the oven to 200°C/180°C fan/400°F/gas mark 6. Line a 900g (2lb) loaf tin approximately 24cm x 14cm (9½in x 5½in) with baking paper.

Mix together the flour, baking powder, salt, sugar and desiccated (shredded) coconut in a mixing bowl. Combine the coconut milk, eggs, vanilla extract and melted butter in a jug, mix well, then slowly pour the liquid ingredients into the dry ingredients. Mix well between additions to form a smooth batter.

Pour the batter into the prepared loaf tin and bake for 45 minutes–1 hour. Allow to cool a little on a wire rack before turning out and slicing.

To make the raspberry cream, beat the crème fraîche and the mascarpone in a bowl. Gently mix through a spoonful of the raspberry jam (jelly) to give a ripple effect.

When you're ready to eat, toast the bread in a dry pan, spread over a little jam and top with the raspberry cream and fresh raspberries.

DUTCH BABY WITH FIGS AND RASPBERRIES

Serves 4

A cross between a pancake and a Yorkshire pudding, this epic breakfast or brunch dish is an American creation with Germanic roots. You often see it served in the cast-iron skillet it's cooked in. I'm using figs and raspberries here, but it can be adorned with anything you feel like adding. It also makes a great edible serving bowl for scoops of vanilla ice cream, maple syrup and toasted pecans.

For the batter
125g (4½oz) plain
    (all-purpose) flour
125ml (4fl oz) full-fat (whole) milk
3 medium free-range eggs
Pinch of ground cinnamon
Small pinch of freshly
    grated nutmeg
Pinch of fine salt
30g (1oz) salted butter

For the fig and raspberry filling
25g (1oz) salted butter
4 ripe black figs, sliced
    horizontally
1–2 tsp caster (superfine) sugar
3–4 tbsp Marsala wine (optional)
350g (12oz) raspberries

To serve
150g (5½oz) crème fraîche
Icing (confectioners') sugar,
    for dusting

Preheat the oven to 220°C/200°C fan/425°F/gas mark 7.

Mix the flour, milk, eggs, cinnamon, nutmeg and salt together in a large bowl.

Heat the 30g (1oz) butter in a 25cm (10in) cast-iron pan (skillet). When it's good and hot, pour in the batter. Transfer to the oven and cook for 20 minutes, or until risen and golden.

In the meantime, to make the fig and raspberry filling, melt the 25g (1oz) butter in a large frying pan (skillet) over a medium heat. Add the figs and the sugar and warm gently over a low-medium heat for about 5 minutes, to warm the fruit through and soften it a little. (If using the Marsala, add it to the pan now, turn up the heat a bit and simmer until the volume of the liquid is reduced by half.) Remove from the heat and stir in the raspberries. Set aside.

To serve, fill the risen Dutch baby with the warm fruit and any juices from the pan. Serve with crème fraîche and a dusting of icing (confectioners') sugar.

FLATBREADS WITH MASHED AVOCADO, POACHED EGGS, CHILLI, PRESERVED LEMON AND PINE NUTS

Serves 2

A great brunch dish for those seeking their morning avocado kick. The preserved lemon and chilli wakes up the whole dish – kind of what you need in the morning.

These quick flatbreads are a real asset, as there's no waiting for yeast to rise or dough to prove, so you can knock them up at the last minute.

For the flatbreads
200g (7oz) self-raising flour, plus extra for dusting
200g (7oz) full-fat Greek yoghurt
½ tsp bicarbonate of soda (baking soda)
Pinch of fine salt
Sea salt and freshly ground black pepper
2 medium free-range eggs, poached (see page 12), kept warm, to serve

For the mashed avocado
1 ripe avocado, peeled, stoned and chopped
Juice of 1 lime
1 tsp chopped tarragon
1 tsp chopped dill

For the cucumber salad
½ cucumber, cut into long batons
30g (1 oz) lamb's lettuce or watercress
2 tbsp olive oil
Juice of ½ lemon
Pinch of black onion seeds

For the chilli, preserved lemon and pine nuts
¼ tsp dried chilli flakes
2 preserved lemons, chopped (I use small ones from a jar)
1 tsp sesame seeds, toasted in a dry pan
1 tsp fennel seeds, toasted in a dry pan and crushed in a pestle and mortar
1 tbsp pine nuts, toasted in a dry pan and chopped

First make the flatbreads: combine all the ingredients in a large bowl, mixing together until it forms a soft dough. Divide the dough in half. Flour a work surface and roll out the dough to form 2 x 20cm (8in) rounds about 5mm (¼in) thick.

Heat a large frying pan (skillet) over a high heat and cook the flatbreads on each side for 3–4 minutes until blistered and cooked through. Keep somewhere warm until you're ready to serve.

Mash the avocado in a bowl with the lime juice and herbs, and season with salt and pepper.

Next, mix all the salad ingredients in a bowl to combine.

Finally, mix the ingredients for the chilli, preserved lemon and pine nuts together in a bowl.

To serve, spread the mashed avocado onto the warm flatbreads and then top each with a warm poached egg. Spoon over the cucumber salad and then sprinkle over the chilli, lemon and pine nuts.

Breakfast and Brunch

NASI LEMAK

Serves 4

Nasi lemak, the breakfast of kings! This national dish of Malaysia is a spicy coconut rice eaten for breakfast, served with a fiery hot sambal to accompany it. If it feels a little too early in the day, it makes a great brunch dish for later.

There might be a few ingredients here that are new to you. Some of them are available from larger supermarkets, or you should be able to find them online. The flavour of the finished dish will be worth going the extra mile.

For the nasi lemak
400ml (14fl oz) tin coconut milk
5cm (2in) piece root ginger, finely chopped
1 lemongrass stick, smashed with the back of a knife
350g (12oz) basmati rice
½ tsp sea salt
400ml (14fl oz) water
2 banana leaves (available from some Asian grocers), to serve

For the sambal
2 tbsp vegetable oil
2 shallots, thinly sliced
2 garlic cloves, finely chopped
1 tsp fermented shrimp paste
2 tsp gochujang (a bright-red Korean fermented chilli paste)
110g (3½oz) dried anchovies (also sold as ikan bilis; you can use dried shrimps if unavailable), soaked in water and drained
2 tbsp palm sugar
250ml (9fl oz) jarred tamarind paste
Juice of 1 lime

For the garnish
Vegetable oil, for frying
60g (2¼oz) dried anchovies (see above)
4 medium free-range eggs, soft-boiled and shells removed
75g (2½oz) unsalted peanuts, toasted in a dry pan
⅓ cucumber, thinly sliced

Start by putting the coconut milk, ginger, lemongrass, rice and sea salt in a large saucepan. Add the water, mix well and cook over a medium heat for 15–20 minutes. When it's cooked, all the liquid will have been absorbed into the rice.

For the sambal, heat a frying pan (skillet) over a medium heat and add the oil. Once hot, add the shallots and garlic to the pan and cook, stirring, for 5 minutes, or until soft.

Add the shrimp paste and gochujang and almost all the soaked anchovies (reserve some for the garnish) and stir. Add the sugar and the tamarind and simmer for 1–2 minutes. Using a stick blender, whizz the sambal to a coarse relish-like consistency, and loosen with 60–150ml (2–5fl oz) water if it's too thick. Stir in the lime juice off the heat and set aside.

To make the garnish, heat a 2cm (¾in) layer of vegetable oil in a heavy-based pan. When the oil is hot enough to brown a small cube of bread in 40–50 seconds, add the dried anchovies to the pan and cook for 2 minutes, or until crisp and golden brown. Remove using a slotted spoon and drain on a plate lined with paper towels.

To serve, divide the rice evenly between four serving bowls (discard the lemongrass) and press the rice down until it is compacted. Upturn the rice bowls in the middle of the banana leaves. Arrange the halved eggs, toasted peanuts, cucumber and remaining anchovies around the rice and sprinkle with the crispy fried anchovies.

EGGS AND THINGS

Serves 1

Here are four different ways to enjoy your breakfast or brunch eggs – or feel free to experiment and make up your own versions.

For the eggs and things
Vegetable oil, for frying
3 medium free-range eggs
Small knob of butter
Sea salt and cracked
    black pepper
Crusty bread or hot toast,
    to serve

Miso butter and shallots
2 tbsp olive oil
2 small round shallots, halved
1 heaped tbsp miso
30g (1oz) unsalted butter, softened
1–2 tbsp water
2 tbsp chopped chives

**Salami, potato and
Gruyère cheese**
1 tbsp olive oil
20g (¾oz) unsalted butter
1 medium potato, peeled and cut
    into small dice
4 slices of salami
20g (¾oz) Gruyère cheese, grated

**Salmon, crème fraîche, Dijon
and tarragon**
2 slices of smoked salmon,
    chopped
1–2 tbsp crème fraîche
2 tsp Dijon mustard
1 tsp chopped tarragon leaves
Juice of ½ lemon

**Blackened asparagus and
chorizo vinaigrette**
1 tbsp olive oil
1 small chorizo sausage, chopped
20g (¾oz) stale breadcrumbs
3 asparagus spears, cut in half
    lengthways
Splash of red wine
    or sherry vinegar

Take a small non-stick frying pan (skillet) and add a little vegetable oil. When the oil is hot, crack in the eggs and fry gently for a few minutes before adding a knob of butter to the pan and seasoning with cracked black pepper. Baste in the seasoned butter, spooning it over the eggs for a few minutes to crisp them around the edges and cook the tops.

Top the eggs with whatever you fancy and serve with the crusty bread or hot toast. Here are a few suggestions...

For the **miso butter and shallots**, heat the olive oil in a frying pan over a medium heat, add the halved shallots and cook, stirring, until coloured and soft, about 10 minutes.

Add the miso, butter and the water and simmer for about 5 minutes. Take the pan off the heat, stir through the chives and spoon the sauce over the eggs.

For the **salami, potato and Gruyère cheese**, heat the oil and butter in a frying pan over a medium heat. Add the potato and cook gently until soft, about 5 minutes. Add the sliced salami, stir to heat through, and spoon over the eggs. Top with the grated Gruyère cheese.

For the **salmon, crème fraîche, Dijon and tarragon**, season the smoked salmon with salt and pepper. In a bowl, stir together the crème fraîche, Dijon mustard, chopped tarragon and lemon juice. Lay the salmon on top of the eggs and top with the crème fraîche mix.

For the **blackened asparagus and chorizo vinaigrette**, heat the olive oil in a frying pan over a medium heat. When hot, fry the chorizo, stirring, until crisp, about 5 minutes. Add the stale breadcrumbs and fry for a further 2–3 minutes until crisp. Transfer the chorizo and breadcrumbs to a bowl.

Add the asparagus to the hot pan and season with salt. Turn up the heat to high and fry the asparagus until it is soft and blackened a little, about 10 minutes. Add a splash of red wine or sherry vinegar and a twist of black pepper. Throw the chorizo and crumbs back into the pan to warm through, then spoon over the eggs.

Breakfast and Brunch

WARM SALAD OF SMOKED HADDOCK, BLACK PUDDING AND BACON

Serves 2

My kind of salad! Warm salads are the best sort, and this one is bursting with flavours. It could be a breakfast or brunch dish, or even a light supper. If you want to make it more substantial, you could always add a soft-boiled egg, cut into quarters.

2 tbsp olive oil
8 curry leaves
200g (7oz) thick piece smoked haddock, pin-boned and skin on
1½ tsp Dijon mustard
60ml (2fl oz) plain yoghurt
Pinch of sugar
60ml (2fl oz) crème fraîche
Sea salt

For the salad
1–2 tbsp olive oil
2 salad potatoes, finely diced
50g (1¾oz) thick-cut bacon, finely diced
75g (2½oz) black pudding
50g (1¾oz) mixed salad leaves

Preheat the oven to 200°C/180°C fan/400°F/gas mark 6.

Heat the oil in a medium ovenproof frying pan (skillet) over a high heat. When it's hot, throw in the curry leaves and cook until crisp, 10–20 seconds. As soon as they have stopped spluttering, remove them using a slotted spoon and drain on a plate lined with paper towels.

Season the fish with a pinch of sea salt and place it flesh-side down in the same pan, over a medium heat. Cook gently for around 5 minutes, or until you see a golden crust forming on the bottom. Transfer the pan to the oven for 5–6 minutes to finish cooking.

Mix the Dijon mustard, yoghurt, sugar and crème fraiche in a bowl and set aside.

To make the salad, heat the olive oil in a frying pan over a medium heat, add the potatoes and bacon and fry for 5 minutes. Crumble in the black pudding and cook until crisp and the potatoes and bacon are golden brown, about 10 minutes.

Toss the salad leaves in a serving bowl. Add the black pudding, potato and bacon mixture and mix well.

To serve, spoon the crème fraîche and mustard cream onto warmed serving plates, top with the warm salad, flake over the roasted haddock and scatter with the fried curry leaves.

SUGAR-CURED PRAWNS WITH CRISP BACON AND DEVILLED EGGS

**Serves 4 as a
light starter**

Sugar-curing is a great way to season fish and shellfish. The sugar/salt combination adds bags of flavour, and the curing process also alters the texture, making the flesh deliciously sweet and firm. This dish is my take on a Scandinavian dish that's popular at brunch.

It's best to cure the prawns the day before you plan to eat this dish.

For the sugar-cured prawns
15g (½oz) fine sea salt
80g (2¾oz) caster (superfine) sugar
Small bunch of dill, leaves and
    stalks chopped, a few sprigs
    reserved to garnish
400g (14oz) raw prawns (shrimp),
    peeled and deveined
Freshly ground black pepper

**For the crisp bacon and
devilled eggs**
8 hard-boiled medium free-range
    eggs, peeled
80g (2¾oz) good-quality
    mayonnaise
1 tsp Dijon mustard
3 tbsp crème fraîche
A few drops of Tabasco or other
    hot sauce
1 tsp cayenne pepper
1–2 tbsp vegetable oil
4 slices of best quality unsmoked
    streaky bacon

Mix the salt, sugar and chopped dill in a shallow bowl. Add the prawns and mix well. Cover and refrigerate for 12–24 hours for best results. During this time the prawns will firm up and release a lot of liquid. At the end of the curing time, drain the prawns and discard the liquid.

Heat a ridged griddle pan until hot. When it's nice and hot, add the prawns and cook for 1–2 minutes on each side, or until they turn pink all over. Remove from the heat and set aside.

Carefully cut the boiled eggs in half. Using a teaspoon, remove the yolks and put them in a bowl, keeping the white shells intact. Mix the egg yolks to a smooth paste with the mayonnaise, Dijon mustard, crème fraîche and Tabasco.

Spoon (or pipe) the mixture back into the white shells and sprinkle over the cayenne pepper.

Heat the oil in a frying pan (skillet), add the bacon and fry until crisp on both sides. Transfer to a plate lined with paper towels to drain.

To serve, place the devilled eggs on a serving plate, grind over the black pepper, scatter over the prawns and the dill sprigs and, finally, break over the crisp shards of bacon.

CURRIED POTATO CROQUETTES WITH POACHED EGGS

Serves 4

A great brunch dish that involves little more than some leftover mashed potato and a few eggs. The gluten-free quinoa and seeds mixture makes an interesting, nutty, crunchy coating, a change from the usual breadcrumbs.

For the croquettes
400g (14oz) mashed potato, made from baked potatoes, not boiled, warmed
1 tbsp medium curry powder
1 tsp ground cumin
1 tsp ground coriander
1 tsp ground turmeric
Vegetable oil, for deep-frying
75g (2½oz) chickpea flour
2 medium free-range eggs, beaten
10g (¼oz) black onion seeds
10g (¼oz) coriander seeds
120g (4¼oz) uncooked quinoa
Sea salt and freshly ground black pepper
4 medium free-range eggs, poached, to serve (see page 12)

For the vegetables
2 tbsp olive oil
1 leek, finely chopped
½ head broccoli, broken into small florets
1 pak choi, leaves separated

For the dressing
2 tbsp rapeseed (canola) oil
Juice of 1 lime
½ tsp curry powder
Pinch of black onion seeds
Pinch of coriander seeds, toasted in a dry pan

Start with the croquettes: put the warmed mashed potato in a large bowl, add the curry powder, cumin, coriander and turmeric, season with salt and pepper and mix well to combine. Shape the mixture into 4 even-sized croquettes, then cover and chill in the fridge for 30 minutes.

Preheat a deep-fat fryer to 180°C (350°F), or half-fill a large, deep, heavy-based pan with oil and set over a medium-high heat. The oil is hot enough when a small cube of bread dropped into the oil turns golden brown in 40–50 seconds (or you can test the temperature using a probe thermometer).

Put the chickpea flour in one small bowl, put the beaten eggs in a second small bowl, and the black onion seeds, coriander seeds and quinoa in a third small bowl. Roll each chilled croquette in the flour first, then the egg and, finally, the seeds and quinoa.

Deep-fry the croquettes in the hot oil until golden brown and crisp, 6–8 minutes. Remove the croquettes using a slotted metal spoon and drain on a plate lined with paper towels. Keep warm.

To cook the vegetables, heat the olive oil in a large frying pan (skillet) over a medium heat, add the leek, broccoli and pak choi and cook, stirring, for 2–3 minutes.

Mix all the dressing ingredients together in a small bowl and whisk.

To serve, drizzle the vegetables with the dressing and pile onto a serving plate. Add the croquettes and top with the poached eggs.

Serves 4

Pretty much a storecupboard recipe from start to finish – a well-stocked, adventurous storecupboard, perhaps, but all the same! If you want to 'beef' these up, a handful of rehydrated and chopped dried porcini mushrooms works a treat.

For the burgers

4 tbsp olive oil
1 red onion, finely chopped
1 garlic clove, crushed
1 green chilli, deseeded
    and chopped
1 tsp grated root ginger
2 tbsp coriander (cilantro)
    stalks, chopped
1 tbsp ground coriander
600g (11b 5oz) cooked brown
    lentils, drained and rinsed
3 tbsp chickpea flour
Sea salt and freshly ground
    black pepper

For the carrot and apple pickle

2 large carrots, peeled and cut into
    5cm (2in) lengths and as thin as
    you dare
2 tsp sea salt
¼ cucumber, cut to about the
    same size as the carrots
1 red apple, peeled and cut
    to about the same size
    as the carrots
100g (3½oz) caster
    (superfine) sugar
100ml (3½fl oz) cider vinegar

For the peanut and sesame sauce

2 tbsp smooth peanut butter
2 tbsp full-fat Greek yoghurt
1 tbsp tahini
2 tsp white sesame seeds, toasted
Zest and juice of 1 lemon

To serve

4 burger buns, cut in half
2 beef tomatoes, sliced
1 baby gem lettuce, shredded

First, make the burgers: heat 2 tablespoons of the oil in a large frying pan (skillet) over a high heat and cook the onion, garlic, chilli and ginger, stirring, for 2–3 minutes, or until soft. Add the coriander (cilantro) stalks, ground coriander and lentils and mix well.

Transfer the lentil mixture to a food processor, add the chickpea flour and pulse (do not blend) until the mixture has a chunky texture. Season with salt and pepper.

Divide the mixture evenly and shape into 4 burgers. Chill, covered in the fridge, for at least 30 minutes.

While the burgers are chilling, make the carrot and apple pickle and the peanut and sesame sauce. Put the carrots in a heatproof bowl, sprinkle with the salt and leave for 30 minutes. After that time, rinse off the salt and return the carrots to the bowl. Add the cucumber and apple.

Put the sugar and vinegar in a small saucepan over a medium–high heat and stir until the sugar has dissolved. Pour the hot vinegar and sugar mixture over the vegetables, season with salt and pepper and set aside to cool.

Put all the ingredients for the peanut and sesame sauce in a bowl, add 2 tablespoons of water and mix well.

To cook the burgers, heat the remaining oil in the cleaned-out frying pan over a medium heat. When the oil is hot, add the burgers and cook on both sides for 2–3 minutes, or until crisp on the outside and cooked through (cut one open to check).

To serve, put the peanut and sesame sauce on the base of each burger bun and top with a burger. Then add the tomato, lettuce, carrot and apple pickle, and, lastly, the bun top. Serve any extra pickle and sauce alongside.

Breakfast and Brunch

AMERICAN-STYLE COBB SALAD

Serves 4

Ever popular, the Cobb salad is pretty substantial as salads go. Part of its appeal is in the way it's displayed in the bowl and mixed together at the table.

For the dressing

60g (2¼oz) Roquefort cheese
3½ tbsp buttermilk, plus extra
    if needed (you can use
    Greek yoghurt if you can't
    get buttermilk)
1 tbsp mayonnaise
Pinch of ground cumin

For the salad

½ Cos lettuce, chopped
1 red chicory (endive), chopped
2 hard-boiled medium
    free-range eggs, peeled and
    roughly chopped
1 cooked chicken breast,
    thinly sliced
1 ripe avocado, peeled, stoned
    and chopped
4 ripe plum tomatoes, chopped
4 spring onions (scallions),
    chopped
2 tbsp finely chopped fresh mixed
    herbs, such as tarragon, chives
    and parsley
4 slices of smoked streaky
    bacon, cooked to a crisp
    and roughly chopped

To make the dressing, blend all of the ingredients in a food processor. You might need to add extra buttermilk or water if it's too thick. It should have the consistency of pouring cream (light cream).

Arrange the lettuce and chicory (endive) around a large serving dish or platter. Arrange the remaining ingredients in concentric circles, finishing with a sprinkling of herbs and chopped bacon.

Drizzle over the dressing to serve. Mix well at the table just before you dive in.

Historically, in the UK we haven't done barbecues particularly well. We have come a long way in recent years, largely because of the marvellous explosion of good street food in this country. South African braais, and the wood-fired asado feasts of South America are becoming more familiar.

The cuts of meat we use are changing too — it's no longer just economy burgers and multi-packs of chicken drumsticks, but big slow-cooked pieces of beef, maybe a whole fish, assorted vegetables buried in the ashes to char... Now more than ever, eating outside is to be celebrated, and the British barbecue can be lauded rather than laughed at — if the weather permits, of course!

Weekend lunches, whether barbecued or cooked inside, are my absolute favourite way to entertain, usually starting soon after midday and finishing whenever. I love it when lunch blends into dinner, or 'linner' as we call it. My friend Mitch Tonks says, 'A great lunch starts at 1pm and ends in Monte Carlo a week later.'

I love the endless sharing plates, long, messy tables laden with food, empty wine bottles quickly replaced by more. I love hearty, fuss-free dishes that don't stand on ceremony and, ideally, a group of friends who don't require that either. This is the way a great lunch should be spent. With a little bit of pre-planning, you can sit and enjoy it all with your guests.

Lunch and BBQ

SESAME AND SALTED CUCUMBER WITH BASIL, AVOCADO AND WATERCRESS

**Serves 2
generously
or 4 as side**

1 cucumber
½ tsp sea salt
1 avocado, peeled and stoned
1 garlic clove, chopped
Juice of 2 limes
1 tsp toasted sesame oil
100g (3½oz) edamame beans
3 spring onions (scallions),
    chopped
1 bunch of basil, leaves torn
Olive oil, for drizzling
Sea salt and freshly ground
    black pepper

To serve
50g (1¾oz) dressed
    watercress leaves
1 tbsp toasted white
    sesame seeds

A light and punchy summer salad, packed full of flavour.

Smashing the cucumber is very therapeutic, but it does also serve the purpose of getting the seeds removed quickly, which can otherwise make the salad a bit wet.

Put the cucumber on a chopping board and smash it repeatedly using something heavy, like a rolling pin. Fun, isn't it? Next, pull it apart into irregular chunks and remove and discard the seeds.

Toss the cucumber into a colander, add the sea salt and allow to sit for 30 minutes to soften, then transfer to a bowl.

Meanwhile, blend or crush by hand the avocado, garlic, most of the lime juice and the sesame oil in a bowl. Taste, and season with salt (if needed) and pepper.

Toss the edamame beans with the cucumber, adding the spring onions (scallions) and basil leaves. Add a drizzle of olive oil and some more lime juice and season.

To serve, spoon the mashed avocado onto a serving plate, scatter over the cucumber and edamame bean mixture and add some dressed watercress. Scatter over the toasted sesame seeds.

Serves 4
as a side

Quinoa has a reputation for being a bit dull, and that's because it is! So here I've jazzed it up with a lot of other ingredients and finished it with a spicy dressing. This would make a good accompaniment for grilled merguez sausages or barbecued chicken.

For the quinoa salad
100g (3½oz) quinoa
200ml (7fl oz) vegetable stock
100g (3½oz) kale, shredded
Juice of 1 lemon
Olive oil, for drizzling
240g (8½oz) tinned
    chickpeas, drained
100g (3½oz) cooked puy lentils
100g (3½oz) cashews, toasted in
    a dry pan and roughly chopped
Sea salt and freshly ground
    black pepper

For the dressing
4 tbsp olive oil
2 garlic cloves, finely chopped
2 tbsp finely chopped
    oregano leaves
¼ tsp English mustard powder
¼ tsp ground coriander
125g (4½oz) piri-piri sauce
1 tbsp red wine vinegar

To serve
20g (¾oz) sunflower seeds
10g (¼oz) sesame seeds
20g (¾oz) pumpkin seeds

Put the quinoa in a dry frying pan (skillet) and cook over a high heat for 10 minutes or so until the grains start to brown and pop. Pour over the stock, turn down the heat and cook gently for around 30 minutes until soft.

Put the kale in a large bowl and squeeze over the lemon juice, season well with salt and pepper and add a drizzle of olive oil. Using your hands, scrunch the kale vigorously for a minute to start to soften and break down the otherwise scratchy leaves. Leave to macerate for 10 minutes.

Add the kale, chickpeas, lentils and cashews to the cooked quinoa and mix well.

To make the piri-piri dressing, heat the oil in a medium saucepan and, once hot, add the garlic and cook for 1–2 minutes, stirring. Add the oregano, mustard powder, ground coriander, piri-piri sauce and vinegar and cook for 1–2 minutes.

To serve, toast the seeds in a dry, hot frying pan for 2–3 minutes, stirring continuously. Arrange the salad on a serving plate, pour the dressing over the salad and sprinkle with the seeds.

WHIPPED FETA WITH BLACKENED SPRING ONIONS, CHILLI DRESSING AND DILL

Serves 2
as a starter

50g (1¾oz) feta cheese, crumbled
3½ tbsp double (heavy) cream
Sea salt and freshly ground
    black pepper

For the dressing
12 spring onions (scallions),
    around 2 bunches
½ tsp sea salt
2 tbsp olive oil
1 tsp chilli flakes
1 garlic clove, chopped

To serve
Zest and juice of 1 lime
½ bunch of dill, chopped

Searing them in a dry pan over a high heat is a great way to cook spring onions (scallions). The dry, intense heat gives you that charred, barbecue taste, even from your kitchen stove. This dish works well as a light starter or as part of a mezze selection.

Whizz the feta and double (heavy) cream in a food processor until smooth. Season with salt and set aside in a bowl.

Put a dry frying pan (skillet) over a high heat and when it's very hot, lay the dry spring onions in the pan and sprinkle the ½ tsp sea salt over them. Press down on the onions using another smaller, heavier pan, lifting the top pan every now and again to check on the spring onions. You want them to cook and soften while they char in the dry pan. This will take 10–15 minutes.

In a small pan, heat the olive oil, chilli flakes and garlic over a low heat for 1–2 minutes to bring out the flavour, without burning the garlic.

To serve, spoon the whipped feta onto a serving dish, top with the blackened spring onions and spoon over the chilli dressing. Season with salt and pepper, squeeze over the lime juice and sprinkle over the lime zest and dill.

WARM HALLOUMI WITH WATERMELON, PARMA HAM AND HERBS

Serves 2

1 x 250g (9oz) block
   good-quality halloumi
   cheese, still in its packet
2 slices of stale crusty bread,
   torn into chunks
2 tbsp sherry vinegar
3 tbsp extra virgin olive oil
2 thick slices of watermelon, cut
   into 8cm (3in) chunks
1 tbsp olive oil
4 slices of Parma ham
½ small bunch of mint leaves
1 handful of basil leaves
1 handful of flatleaf parsley leaves
Sea salt and freshly ground
   black pepper

Some time ago I visited a halloumi producer in Cyprus. I was never a big fan of this cheese until then, but the producer showed me the best way to eat it – straight from the warm salted brine it sits in. It was a revelation, and the resulting texture is totally unlike the dry grilled stuff. It'll change your life!

Bring a pan of water to the boil then add the halloumi, still in its plastic packet. Turn down the heat and let the cheese simmer for 20 minutes to warm through and soften. Remove from the water and allow to cool before opening.

While the halloumi is cooling, put the bread chunks in a bowl and drizzle over the sherry vinegar and 2 tablespoons of the olive oil. Allow to sit and soak for 10 minutes, then toss together. Drizzle the remaining olive oil over the watermelon and season with salt and pepper.

Arrange the watermelon chunks on a serving dish, lay the ham slices on top, then scatter over the mint, basil and parsley. Open the packet of halloumi and drain off the liquid. Tear the halloumi into chunks and add to the salad to serve.

CRAB SCONES WITH APPLE AND FENNEL SALAD

Makes 8

360g (12¾oz) plain
    (all-purpose) flour
10g (¼oz) baking powder
100g (3½oz) cold salted butter,
    cut into cubes
40g (1½oz) strong Cheddar, grated
Pinch of cayenne pepper
1 tsp fennel seeds, toasted
    and lightly crushed in a pestle
    and mortar
Zest of 1 lemon
100g (3½oz) brown crabmeat
170ml (5½fl oz) full-fat (whole) milk
1 medium free-range egg, beaten
Sea salt and freshly ground
    black pepper
75g (2½oz) salted butter, softened,
    to serve

For the salad
½ fennel bulb with fronds,
    thinly sliced
½ green apple, thinly sliced
2 tbsp white crabmeat
2 tbsp cider vinegar
Pinch of caster (superfine) sugar
3 tbsp olive oil
Juice of 1 lemon
1 tbsp torn dill or chervil

Brown crabmeat is often overlooked but this is where all the best flavour is. These scones are a doddle to make and are pretty impressive as a snack or starter. Double up the ingredients if you're going to make them, because they won't last long!

Preheat the oven to 200°C/180°C fan/400°F/gas mark 6. Line a baking tray with baking paper.

Briefly blitz the flour, baking powder and butter in a food processor to create a breadcrumb texture. Or, to make it by hand, put the ingredients in a large mixing bowl and rub the butter into the flour and baking powder.

If using a processor, tip the mixture into a large bowl. Add the cheese, cayenne pepper, fennel seeds, lemon zest and crabmeat and form a dough by mixing well while slowly adding the milk. Wrap in cling film (plastic wrap) and chill in the fridge for an hour.

Roll out or press the dough with your hands to a 2.5cm (1in) thickness and use a 6cm (2½in) cutter to cut out about 8 rounds. Put on the lined baking tray, brush with the beaten egg and bake for 10–15 minutes. Set aside to cool on a wire rack.

To make the salad, toss together the sliced fennel, apple and crabmeat in a bowl with a pinch of salt.

In a separate bowl, whisk together the vinegar, sugar, oil and lemon juice.

Just before serving add the dressing to the salad and mix gently to coat. Sprinkle with the dill or chervil. Serve the warm scones with plenty of butter, with the salad alongside.

Serves 6

This recipe is a nod to a dish I was introduced to many years ago, from Mantua in northern Italy. Sweet, spicy, citrus and sour flavours enliven a simple poached chicken, and the accompanying parsley salad makes it the perfect summer lunchtime dish.

For the poached chicken
325ml (11fl oz) decent-quality
   dry white wine
5 tbsp white wine vinegar
7–8cm (3in) piece cinnamon stick
2 bay leaves
1 tbsp black peppercorns
1 tbsp coriander seeds
1 orange, zested in strips and
   juiced (keep the juice for
   the dressing)
1 lemon, zested in strips and
   juiced (keep the juice for the
   dressing)
1 large (1.5–2kg/3½lb–4½lb)
   chicken
Sea salt and freshly ground
   blackpepper

For the dressing
3½ tbsp red wine vinegar
1 tsp caster (superfine) sugar
3½ tbsp olive oil
2 tbsp pine nuts, toasted
   in a dry pan
Reserved juice from the orange
   and lemon

For the parsley salad
4 tbsp bulgur wheat
300ml (10½fl oz) water
100g (3½oz) flatleaf parsley,
   finely chopped
2 garlic cloves, grated
½ red onion, chopped
2 beef tomatoes, chopped
2 tbsp chopped mint leaves
4 tbsp olive oil
Seeds from ½ pomegranate,
   to serve

Bring a large pan of salted water to a boil and add all the poaching ingredients apart from the chicken itself. When the water is boiling, carefully add the chicken to the water and bring it back to the boil. As soon as the water begins to boil, reduce the heat to low, so that there is only a very gentle blip on the surface.

Poach for at least 1 hour (the exact time will depend on the size of the chicken). After 1 hour, try gently tugging on one of the legs. If the leg comes away easily from the body, the chicken is cooked. If the leg still shows some resistance, give it another 15–20 minutes and check again. Once it's cooked, allow the chicken to cool in the stock.

When cool enough to handle, remove the bird from the poaching liquid, strip the meat from the bones (discard the skin and bones) and put it in a large bowl. Reserve 100ml (3½fl oz) of the poaching liquid. (You can use the rest of the poaching liquid for another dish, or freeze it for future use.)

To make the dressing, warm the vinegar and caster (superfine) sugar in a small pan over a low heat until the sugar has dissolved, then add the olive oil and mix well. Pour the warm dressing over the shredded chicken, then add the pine nuts, some of the reserved citrus juice to taste and a few tablespoons of the reserved poaching liquid and mix well. Taste and season with salt and pepper.

Next, put the bulgur wheat in a dry frying pan (skillet) over a medium heat and cook, stirring, until golden and toasted. Add the 300ml (10½fl oz) water and cook, stirring occasionally, until the bulgur wheat is soft, about 15 minutes. Drain and set aside to cool.

Mix all the parsley salad ingredients together in a bowl, then add the cooled bulgur wheat and mix well. Taste and season.

To serve, mix the shredded, dressed chicken and the parsley salad together in a large serving bowl and garnish with the pomegranate seeds.

Lunch and BBQ

Lunch and BBQ

MEXICAN-STYLE GRILLED CORN

Serves 2

2 corn on the cob
1 tbsp vegetable oil
2 tbsp good-quality mayonnaise
1 tsp smoked paprika
1 tsp chilli flakes
100g (3½oz) feta cheese or good
   crumbly Cheddar
1 lime, cut into quarters

I first tasted this from a street vendor's stall in San Cristóbal, a beautiful hilltop town in southern Mexico. It was one of those standout moments from a very eventful trip. Such a simple street food but utterly delicious and easily re-created at home.

Get a barbecue good and hot, or preheat the grill (broiler) to high. When hot, brush the corn with the oil and barbecue or grill (broil) for 10–15 minutes, turning regularly, until to softened and blistered all over.

Brush with mayonnaise and dust with the smoked paprika and chilli flakes.

Crumble the cheese over the corn, squeeze over some lime quarters and serve immediately.

BARBECUED BROCCOLI WITH HONEY AND BLUE CHEESE DRESSING

Serves 4

1 tbsp olive oil
400g (14oz) Tenderstem
    broccoli spears
Sea salt and freshly ground
    black pepper

For the dressing
1 tsp runny honey
1 tsp wholegrain mustard
1 tbsp cider vinegar
3 tbsp rapeseed (canola) oil

To serve
150g (5½oz) soft blue cheese
300ml (10½fl oz) double
    (heavy) cream
2 tbsp fresh breadcrumbs,
    fried in a little butter

Broccoli works well here, but large spring onions (scallions) or baby leeks would work too. Charring over coals gives an unrivaled smoky taste, but failing that, a stovetop chargrill gives good results. If you splash a little water over the broccoli as it cooks, the steam produced will help to keep the vegetables moist so they don't dry out.

Lightly oil and season the broccoli with salt and pepper. Place over the coals of a hot grill and cook for 5 minutes or so until blackened and tender. Alternatively, heat a large ridged griddle pan until hot and char the broccoli. Splash a little water over the broccoli as it cooks. The steam produced will help to keep the broccoli moist.

Mix all the dressing ingredients together in a bowl and, once the broccoli is charred and just before serving, dress the broccoli.

Put the soft blue cheese in a medium bowl and beat together with the cream until it's smooth and has a drizzling consistency. You can use a large whisk or a wooden spoon for this.

Scatter the dressed broccoli onto a serving dish. Sprinkle over the fried breadcrumbs and drizzle the heads of the broccoli with the blue cheese cream. Alternatively just dip the broccoli into the cream – perfect finger food!

GRILLED LANGOUSTINES WITH SESAME SEED DRESSING

Serves 2

Langoustines are without doubt one of the most delicious things that we don't eat enough of in this country, possibly because of the cost but also because of the fiddliness of eating. They are a real treat, and one to be lingered over. Half the pleasure is really in the theatre of sitting down to a plateful of these beauties and getting stuck in. The discarded shells and claws (there's a lot of sweet meat in these) can be saved to make soup and stock, so nothing is wasted. British shellfish is the envy of the world and we should celebrate it more.

16 live langoustines
Olive oil, for drizzling
Pinch of salt

For the sesame seed dressing
1 banana shallot, chopped
5cm (2in) piece root ginger,
    peeled and grated
1 garlic clove, finely chopped
1 small green chilli, deseeded
    and chopped
4 tbsp light soy sauce
4 tbsp rice wine vinegar
4 tbsp toasted sesame oil
6 spring onions (scallions),
    chopped
Sea salt and freshly ground
    black pepper

To garnish and serve
40g (1½oz) fresh watercress
    or rocket (arugula)
1 tsp white sesame seeds,
    toasted in a dry pan

Preheat a grill (broiler) to high.

Start by blanching the langoustines in boiling salted water for 4 minutes. Lift out using a pair of kitchen tongs and place on a tray or rack to cool.

Using a heavy knife, cut the langoustines in half from head to tail. Drizzle with olive oil, season with salt and place under the grill for 1–2 minutes.

Mix all the dressing ingredients together in a bowl, taste and season with salt and pepper.

To serve, arrange the watercress or rocket (arugula) on a large platter, pile the grilled langoustines on top, spoon over the dressing and sprinkle over the sesame seeds.

ROASTED RED MULLET WITH BASIL AND SUN-DRIED TOMATO AND CHILLI TOAST

Serves 2

Red mullet has a strong, distinctive flavour and an interesting texture, and it stands up well to punchy herbs. It's thought of as a Mediterranean fish, so it goes well with the associated flavours in this dish. Often red mullet are sold with the liver still intact. This is highly prized and is similar to a chicken liver, creamy and delicious. If you're lucky enough to get some, fry them up and serve them alongside the dish.

2–3 tbsp olive oil, plus
    extra for frying
1 banana shallot, chopped
1 garlic clove, finely chopped
½ bunch of fresh basil, chopped
1 tbsp chopped flatleaf parsley
20g (¾oz) salted butter, softened
2 large red mullet, filleted and
    pin-boned
Pinch of flaked sea salt
Ready-made green salad, to serve

**For the sun-dried tomato
and chilli toast**
¼ baguette, day-old
    preferably, sliced
Olive oil, for drizzling
280g (10oz) jar sun-dried
    tomatoes in oil, drained and
    finely chopped
2 red finger chillies, deseeded
    and finely chopped
Sea salt and freshly ground
    black pepper

Preheat the oven to 200°C/180°C fan/400°F/gas mark 6.

Heat the olive oil in a saucepan over a low heat. When hot, add the shallot and garlic, cover with the lid and sweat for around 10 minutes until soft.

Transfer to a bowl and allow to cool completely before adding the chopped herbs and the butter. Mix together well and set aside.

To make the sun-dried tomato and chilli toast, drizzle the sliced baguette with oil and season with salt and pepper. Place on a baking tray and cook in the oven for 10 minutes, or until golden brown and toasted. Set aside.

Chop the sun-dried tomatoes and chillies together finely, almost to a paste, and add just enough oil, left over from the jar, to bind to a sauce.

For the mullet, check the fillets for small bones and remove them. Spread the herb butter evenly over the fillets. Sandwich them together and chill in the fridge for 10 minutes to firm up the butter.

Heat an ovenproof non-stick frying pan (skillet) and add a drizzle of oil. Season the skin of the fish with flaked sea salt and cook skin-side down for a few minutes each side. Transfer the pan to the oven and cook for 3–4 minutes to finish the cooking.

Serve the red mullet with a green salad and the tomato and chilli toasts.

SMOKY SPRING CHICKEN WITH SWEETCORN AND MANGO SALSA AND BUTTERMILK SAUCE

Serves 2

A spring chicken (or poussin) of this size makes a great supper for two people, because each gets a bit of both the leg (the best bit) and the breast meat. These little birds are so succulent and tender and when partnered with this cooling, zesty Mexican-style salsa and a spoon or two of the sweet, sour, hot sauce, makes a great, relaxed supper dish. This would also be a bloody triumph cooked on the grill in the summer months. You will need to marinate the chicken the day before.

For the smoky chicken
2 spring chickens (poussins),
    around 400g (14oz) each
4 tbsp olive oil
1 tsp ground cumin
2 tsp garlic powder
1 tsp hot smoked paprika
Lime wedges, to serve
Sea salt and freshly ground
    black pepper

**For the sweetcorn and
mango salsa**
2 corn on the cob
1 tbsp vegetable oil
½ red onion, finely chopped
1 ripe mango, peeled, stoned
    and finely diced
1 green chilli, thinly sliced
¼ cucumber, finely diced
1 avocado, peeled, stoned and
    finely chopped
½ bunch of coriander (cilantro),
    finely chopped
Juice of 1 lime
1 garlic clove, finely chopped

For the buttermilk sauce
2 tsp chipotle chilli paste
2 tsp white wine vinegar
2 tsp soft light brown sugar
100ml (3½fl oz) buttermilk
    (or use plain yoghurt)
2 tbsp mayonnaise
Juice of ½ lime

Begin by spatchcocking the birds (removing the backbone and flattening them out). Put the chickens upside-down on a chopping board. Using kitchen scissors, cut firmly down either side of the backbone, remove the bone and discard. Turn the chickens right-side up then flatten firmly with the heel of your hand. Tuck the wings and legs behind the birds.

Place the spatchcocked chickens in a large shallow bowl. In a small bowl, mix together the oil, cumin, garlic powder and paprika. Pour this mixture over the chickens and rub the marinade all over the birds until fully coated. Cover and marinate in the fridge overnight.

Heat a frying pan (skillet) large enough to cook both chickens over a high heat. Place the birds breast-side up in the pan and cook for 5–10 minutes. Turn the chickens over, place a heavy weight, such as another heavy frying pan, on top and allow to cook over a medium heat for 30–40 minutes.

Alternatively, you can cook the chickens in a preheated oven at 200°C/180°C fan/400°F/gas mark 6 for 30–40 minutes.

Rest the birds, covered, for at least 20 minutes.

While the chickens are cooking, make the sweetcorn and mango salsa. Brush the corn on the cob with the vegetable oil and heat a ridged griddle pan over a high heat. Cook the corn, turning frequently, until it is charred all over. This will take 15–20 minutes.

Once cool enough to handle, use a sharp knife to remove the kernels from the cobs and transfer them to a bowl. Add the remaining salsa ingredients, mix well and season with salt and pepper.

For the buttermilk sauce, put all the ingredients in a bowl, mix, and season with salt and pepper.

Serve the cooked chickens on a serving platter and spoon the salsa over. Serve with lime wedges on the side and the buttermilk sauce in a separate small bowl.

SALT AND PEPPER LAMB CHOPS

Serves 4

2 tbsp olive oil
16 x 100g (3½oz) lamb chops
Sea salt and freshly ground
  black pepper

For the seasoning mix
½ tbsp Sichuan peppercorns
1 tbsp fennel seeds
1 tbsp coriander seeds
Pinch of chilli flakes
2 tbsp white sesame seeds
2 sheets of nori seaweed,
  toasted in a dry pan, then
  roughly crumbled
½ tbsp sea salt flakes
1 tbsp caster (superfine) sugar

These salty, spicy lamb chops are the perfect thing to graze on during a leisurely summer's lunch in the garden. Serve with a bucket of ice-cold beers and a good chilled playlist.

To make the seasoning mix, toast the Sichuan peppercorns, fennel seeds, coriander seeds and chilli flakes in a dry pan over a medium heat until you can smell the aromas given off. Tip into a spice grinder or pestle and mortar and pound to a fine powder. Add the sesame seeds, crumbled nori, sea salt flakes and sugar and mix (don't grind).

Heat the oil in a frying pan (skillet) and season the chops well with salt and pepper. When the pan is good and hot, add the lamb chops and sear for 2–3 minutes on each side to keep them pink on the inside.

Transfer the chops to a warmed serving plate and sprinkle over the seasoning mix. Allow to rest for 5–10 minutes before tucking in and demolishing.

REUBEN SANDWICH

Serves 2

The Reuben is one of the all-time American greats. Stuffed full to bursting, it's difficult to eat, but you must dive straight into it without ceremony. It's pretty filthy, but just sensational. Bread and butter pickles are a classic American-style pickled cucumber (nothing to do with bread or butter) with a sweet/sour tang, and the ideal accompaniment.

For the bread and butter pickles
¼ cucumber, about 8–10cm
  (3¼–4in), thinly sliced
½ white onion, sliced
1 tsp sea salt
1 tsp celery seeds
1 tbsp yellow mustard seeds
Pinch of ground turmeric
250ml (9fl oz) cider vinegar
200g (7oz) caster
  (superfine) sugar

For the sauce
4 tbsp mayonnaise
2 tbsp tomato ketchup
A few drops of Tabasco
2 tsp Worcestershire sauce
1 banana shallot, chopped
2 tsp sweet smoked paprika

For the Reuben sandwich
4 slices of rye bread
Knob of softened butter,
  for spreading
8 large slices of deli-counter
  corned beef, thinly sliced
8 slices of Swiss cheese
4 tbsp deli-counter sauerkraut
Sea salt and freshly ground
  black pepper

Make the bread and butter pickles by putting the cucumber, onion and salt in a shallow glass or ceramic bowl, and setting aside for 1–2 hours in the fridge. After that time, rinse the cucumber and onion in cold water and transfer to a bowl.

Put the celery seeds, mustard seeds, turmeric, vinegar and sugar in a medium pan with 100ml (3½fl oz) water and bring to the boil, stirring to dissolve the sugar. Allow to cool slightly, then pour the warm pickling liquid over the cucumber and onion in the bowl and set aside.

Place all the sauce ingredients in a bowl and mix well, then season with salt and pepper. Set aside.

Butter the bread slices on just one side (this will be the side you place on the pan).

To build the sandwich, spoon the sauce on the bread first (reserve some to serve with the sandwich), then add the corned beef, cheese and sauerkraut. Top with another slice of rye bread, buttered-side up.

Heat a large ridged griddle pan or frying pan (skillet) over a medium-high heat and place the sandwiches, buttered-side down in the hot pan. Cook the sandwiches for 5 minutes on each side until the bread is golden brown and the cheese has melted.

To serve, cut the sandwiches diagonally and serve on a plate with the pickles on the side. Serve the remaining sauce on the side and have paper napkins at the ready.

DUCK SAUSAGE ROLLS

**Makes
8–10**

2 x 200–250g (7–9oz) duck legs
2 x 320g (11oz) pots of duck fat
200g (7oz) pork mince
    (ground pork), ideally about
    40% fat content
1 garlic clove, finely chopped
2 small banana shallots,
    finely chopped
½ tsp ground allspice
1 tsp ground coriander
1 tsp ground fennel seeds
    (you can grind the whole seeds
    in a mortar and pestle)
250g (9oz) sheet ready-rolled
    puff pastry
1 medium free-range egg, beaten
2 tbsp black sesame seeds
Sea salt and freshly ground
    black pepper
English mustard or Tamarind
    Ketchup (see page 119), to serve

A super-tasty twist on the original all-time favourite.

To confit the duck legs, place them into a baking tray and sprinkle with around 1 tablespoon of salt per duck leg. Leave covered overnight in the fridge. You can always add some aromatics along with the salt – for example, juniper berries, black peppercorns, star anise, cinnamon stick, garlic – at this stage. When ready to confit, wash off the salt and aromatics, if using, and pat dry.

Preheat the oven to 150°C/130°C fan/300°F/gas mark 2.

Place the duck fat into an ovenproof dish and submerge the legs in the fat, it's important that they are completely covered. Cook in the oven for 2½–3 hours, the meat should just melt away from the bone.

Line a baking tray with baking paper.

Chop the cooked duck meat and add to a large bowl with the pork mince (ground pork), garlic, shallots and spices. Season with salt and pepper and mix well.

Unroll the sheet of puff pastry onto a work surface and cut in half lengthways to make two rolls. Spoon half the filling mixture into a long sausage shape along the long edge of the pastry. Fold the top edge of the pastry down over the meat mixture to form a long roll with a seam at one long edge, and press the edges gently together. Repeat for the second roll.

Place the sausage rolls onto the lined baking tray and, using a pastry brush, brush the edges of the pastry with some of the beaten egg, then crimp the edges with the tines of a fork to seal. Brush the remaining beaten egg all over the pastry and scatter over the sesame seeds. Chill in the fridge for 20 minutes.

Preheat the oven to 190°C/170°C fan/375°F/gas mark 5.

Bake the sausage rolls in the oven for about 30 minutes, or until cooked through. Once cooled cut into equal-sized pieces, as big or small as you like. Serve with English mustard or with the Tamarind Ketchup on page 119.

Lunch and BBQ

Makes 1kg
(2lb 4oz) of
dried biltong

I really got into this addictive, tasty snack in South Africa some time ago. You'll find it sold pretty much everywhere, from backwater roadside garages to high-end bars. It's a national food treasure, and it's so easy and rewarding to make it yourself with a few simple ingredients. For foolproof results, get yourself a purpose-made biltong dryer. I'd recommend the 52 Degrees South brand.

Once dried, this meat will keep outside the fridge, somewhere dry and well ventilated, for weeks.

2kg (4lb 8oz) beef silverside
    (rump roast) with a decent
    amount of fat
250ml (9fl oz) cider vinegar
3 tbsp coriander seeds
1 tbsp black peppercorns,
    crushed in a pestle and mortar
1 tbsp chilli flakes (optional)
2 tbsp coarse sea salt
1 tbsp soft brown sugar

Cut the beef into steaks about 1cm (½in) thick and lay them on a baking tray.

Mix the remaining ingredients together in a bowl and rub the mixture all over the meat. Cover the meat and leave in the fridge for 24 hours, turning halfway through that time.

The next day, remove the meat from the tray and pat dry using paper towels, leaving the spice rub on the surface – don't wash anything off.

Hang the meat from butchers' hooks, or by piercing a hole through each piece using a skewer, then hanging the pieces from string in a well-ventilated area (a collapsible wooden clothes dryer works well), preferably with a fan running to keep the air moving. Make sure the pieces of meat are not touching each other. (The best way to dry it is buy yourself a biltong box; see above.)

Let the meat dry slowly for anywhere between 3–5 days, depending upon the meat's thickness and the room conditions. You are looking for it to be dry but not rock-solid, so you can cut it and eat it.

The dried biltong is best served at the end of the day with an ice-cold beer!

BEEF CHEEK BURGERS WITH MUSHROOM MAYO AND PICKLES

Serves 2

Possibly the best and filthiest burger I've ever made! It takes a bit of time and effort as beef cheek needs a long, slow cook to become tender but, believe me, it's well worth it.

For the beef cheek burgers
200–250g (7–9oz) beef cheek
2 tbsp olive oil, plus extra
   if needed
1 onion, finely chopped
1 star anise
1 bay leaf
2 celery sticks, roughly chopped
4 garlic cloves, peeled and
   left whole
Small bunch of thyme
   (reserve 2 sprigs for the
   mayonnaise, below)
440ml (15¼fl oz) can Irish stout
250ml (9fl oz) beef stock
Sea salt and freshly ground
   black pepper

For the mushroom mayonnaise
20g (¾oz) dried trumpet
   mushrooms, soaked until soft
   in warm water, squeezed dry
   and finely chopped
½ garlic clove, grated
1 tbsp mushroom ketchup
   (optional)
1 tbsp finely chopped parsley
2 thyme sprigs, leaves picked and
   finely chopped
50ml (2fl oz) mayonnaise

To serve
2 burger buns, cut in half
   and toasted
4 cornichons, sliced
½ bunch of watercress,
   leaves picked

Preheat the oven to 150°C/130°C fan/300°F/gas mark 2.

Season the beef cheek with salt and pepper. Heat the oil in a heavy-based ovenproof casserole (use one with a lid) over a medium-high heat. Fry the beef cheek on both sides for 5 minutes, or until coloured all over. Remove the beef from the casserole and set aside.

Make sure there is enough oil in the casserole (add a drizzle more if needed), put the casserole back on the hob over a medium heat and add the onion, star anise, bay leaf, celery, garlic and thyme and cook gently for 15–20 minutes. Pour in the stout, turn up the heat and cook, stirring occasionally, until the liquid is reduced by half, 5–10 minutes.

Pour in the beef stock, return the beef cheek to the casserole, cover with the lid and transfer to the oven to cook for 3–4 hours. When it's ready, the beef should be very tender when tested with a knife.

Once the beef is tender, remove the casserole from the oven and remove the beef cheek from the cooking liquid, Set it aside on a plate, covered, to rest.

Return the casserole to the hob over a medium–high heat and reduce the cooking liquid until you have a sauce consistency, 10–15 minutes.

Shred or cut the beef cheek, then put it the casserole with the reduced cooking liquid and keep it warm until ready to serve.

For the mushroom mayonnaise, put all the ingredients in a bowl and mix well. Season with salt and pepper.

When you're ready to eat, spread the bases of the toasted buns with the mushroom mayonnaise. Add watercress, a layer of the shredded beef cheek, a little of the sauce, top with the sliced cornichons and cover with the bun tops.

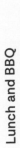

CRUDITÉS WITH ANCHOÏADE

Serves 4
as a starter
or side

½ cucumber, cut into batons
1 small fennel bulb, cut lengthways
    into 8 pieces
2 cooked heritage beetroot
    (beets), peeled and quartered
8 spring onions (scallions), left
    whole but trimmed at each end
8 baby or small carrots, peeled
1 red apple, cut into eighths, core
    removed but not peeled
Handful of breakfast radishes,
    scrubbed and halved
4 celery sticks, taken from the
    heart, with leaves
120g (4¼oz) fine green beans,
    trimmed, blanched and
    refreshed in iced water
4 ripe tomatoes, quartered
1 red and 1 yellow chicory
    (endive), root removed and
    leaves separated
2 hard-boiled medium free-range
    eggs, shelled and quartered

For the anchoïade
2 banana shallots, chopped
1 handful of flatleaf parsley,
    chopped
5 garlic cloves, chopped
60g (2¼oz) anchovy fillets
1–2 tbsp red wine vinegar
150ml (5fl oz) olive oil
Freshly ground black pepper

An easy, speedy dip to enliven any vegetable. If you're an anchovy fan then you'll love this recipe. Anchoïade would also go deliciously well with some grilled lamb chops as part of a summer lunch.

Arrange all the vegetables on a large serving platter, however takes your fancy. I usually group everything into its own section.

To make the anchoïade, put all the ingredients apart from the oil in a food processor and blitz. While the motor is running, slowly add the oil in a thin stream to thicken. Grind in plenty of black pepper and serve with the crudités.

Lunch and BBQ

GRILLED VEGETABLES WITH CRISPY EGG AND ALMOND AND YOGHURT DRESSING

Serves 2

This is a great dish to serve alongside a summer barbecue or similar feast. The vegetables could also be roasted in a very hot oven on a baking tray. Sumac brings a sharp citrus note to the rich deep-fried egg, and adds a great texture.

4 jalapeño chilies, split lengthways in half, seeds knocked out
6 asparagus spears, trimmed
150g (5½oz) sprouting broccoli (broccoli raab), trimmed
100g (3½oz) fine green beans, blanched in boiling salted water and refreshed
6 young carrots, peeled, trimmed, and split in half if too thick
½ lemon, scrubbed and sliced very thinly
6 tbsp olive oil
400g (14oz) tin chickpeas, drained and rinsed
Handful of watercress
Bunch of fresh basil, leaves removed
Handful of rocket (arugula)
60g (2¼oz) salted cashews, toasted and chopped
Sea salt and freshly ground black pepper

For the crispy egg
Vegetable oil, for deep-frying
2 soft-boiled medium free-range eggs, peeled
1 medium free-range egg, beaten
6 tbsp sumac
5 tbsp sesame seeds

For the dressing
3 tbsp almond nut butter
4 tbsp full-fat Greek yoghurt
2 tbsp olive oil
Juice of ½ lemon
1 garlic clove, finely chopped
1 dried ancho chilli, soaked in hot water for 10 minutes then drained and chopped

Start by heating up a barbecue (or large ridged griddle pan) and chargrill the jalapeños, asparagus, broccoli, green beans, carrots and the lemon slices, in batches, if needed, for 4–6 minutes, or until blackened and well cooked. Throw them into a large bowl, add the oil and season with salt and pepper. Add the chickpeas, watercress, basil leaves, rocket (arugula) and cashews and stir together.

For the crispy egg, heat a deep-fat fryer to 180°C (350°F), or half-fill a deep, heavy-based pan with oil set over medium-high heat. The oil is hot enough when a small cube of bread dropped into the oil turns golden brown in 40–50 seconds (or you can test the temperature using a probe thermometer).

Roll the peeled eggs in the beaten egg and then the sumac and sesame seeds. Lower into the hot oil using a slotted metal spoon and cook for 2–3 minutes, or until crispy. Once cooked, remove from the fryer and drain on a plate lined with paper towels.

Mix all the dressing ingredients together. Add 1–2 tablespoons of water or milk to loosen if needed.

Arrange the grilled vegetables on a plate and spoon the almond and yoghurt dressing over the top. Finish with the whole crispy eggs.

JALAPEÑO SALSA

Serves 4

2 corn on the cob
½ onion, finely chopped
Juice of 2 limes
1 garlic clove, crushed
1–2 jalapeños, deseeded and
  finely chopped
2 tbsp finely chopped coriander
  (cilantro)
1 tsp finely chopped oregano
Sea salt and freshly ground
  black pepper

This citrusy, spicy salsa goes brilliantly with the Crispy Beef Tostadas (see page 44) – or equally well with a simple grilled chicken.

Cook the corn on the cob for 10 minutes in a pan of salted, boiling water. It should still have some bite. Remove the corn from the pan and set aside to dry.

Heat a ridged griddle pan until hot then add the corn and char until lightly blackened. Allow to cool. Cut the kernels from the cob using a sharp knife and put them in a large bowl.

Meanwhile, throw the onion in a colander, sprinkle with a heavy seasoning of salt and leave for 10 minutes to soften, and then add to the bowl with the corn. Toss in the lime juice, garlic, jalapeños and herbs, mix well, then taste and season.

ZHOUG DRESSING

Makes
around
300ml

25g (1oz) chopped coriander
  (cilantro)
3 green chillies, deseeded
  and chopped
2 garlic cloves, finely chopped
1 tsp cumin seeds
Juice of 1 lemon
Light olive oil, for drizzling
Pinch of chilli flakes, to serve

This is a fantastic Middle Eastern condiment that will give a powerful kick to anything you fancy to serve with it. It's great spooned over eggs or hummus to enliven a brunch dish, but it also works brilliantly with a simple grilled meat or fish dish.

Put all the ingredients, except the oil and chilli flakes, in a food processor and blend until you have a smooth paste. Drizzle in the oil bit by bit, adding just enough to give you the desired texture. Sprinkle the chilli flakes over the dish you are serving the sauce with for extra heat.

Store the zhoug in a sterilized jar in the fridge for up to 2 weeks.

Weekend

TAMARIND KETCHUP

Makes
700ml

2 tbsp vegetable oil
1 onion, finely chopped
2 garlic cloves, finely chopped
1–2 tbsp cider vinegar
200ml (7fl oz) runny honey
250g (9oz) tamarind paste
8 ripe tomatoes, skinned and
    deseeded (or 400g (14oz)
    tinned tomatoes)
Pinch of ground cloves
1 tsp ground allspice
½ tsp ground cumin
1 cinnamon stick
2 bay leaves
Sea salt and freshly ground
    black pepper

An easy-to-make ketchup that goes really well with the Salmon, Ginger and Chilli Broth (see page 15) or the Pork Banh Mi (see page 33). It would make a tasty addition to barbecued or grilled meats, too.

Heat the oil in a saucepan over a medium heat and add the onion and garlic. Cook, stirring, for 10 minutes to soften.

Add the cider vinegar, honey, tamarind, tomatoes and spices. Season well with salt and pepper, turn the heat down to low and simmer for 20 minutes. Remove from the heat, allow to cool a bit, then remove and discard the cinnamon stick and bay leaf before blending until smooth in a food processor.

Allow to cool, then store in a sterilized jar in the fridge for up to 1 month.

120

Saturday night is the main event. Maybe you've got friends or family round, or maybe there's a birthday or other occasion to celebrate. This is your chance to go all-out and show off a bit, maybe even throw in an extra course or try some new ingredients.

On a Saturday, there's more time to plan, shop and get organized throughout the day. A small amount of planning can make all the difference to whether or not you enjoy the evening as much as your guests.

Tip number one is to aim to make one element of each course spectacular, and everything else alongside it simple – a well-sourced, well-cooked steak served with a simple dressed salad, say, or a beautiful fresh fish, roasted whole and presented with minimal adornment. A couple of nicely cooked scallops served in their shells will steal the show, and a delicate pastry-based dessert needs little else than a dollop of fresh cream. Make life easier for yourself. It's your time to enjoy as well.

Tip number two: don't try to re-create restaurant food – it'll end in tears, and nobody will thank you for your efforts or for the mounds of washing up. Restaurants have lots of trained people on hand to help; home kitchens don't. These recipes will give maximum impact with minimum fuss, and I hope you will find them utterly delicious!

Saturday Night

GRUYÈRE CHEESE, SPINACH AND NUTMEG TART

Serves 6

Gruyère is one of my favourite cheeses and it always makes for a great-tasting tart. It is best served at room temperature to fully appreciate all the nutty, fruity flavours in the cheese.

For the pastry

200g (7oz) plain flour, plus extra for dusting
100g (3½oz) salted butter, diced, plus extra for greasing
1 medium free-range egg

For the filling

4 medium free-range eggs
200ml (7fl oz) double (heavy) cream
200ml (7fl oz) full-fat (whole) milk
25g (1oz) salted butter
230g (8oz) baby spinach
¼ nutmeg, for grating
150g (5½oz) Gruyère cheese, grated
Sea salt and freshly ground black pepper

Grease a 21 x 2.5cm deep (8¼in x 1in deep) tart ring (cake ring) and place on a baking tray lined with baking paper. This will be used for the base of the tart.

For the pastry, using a food processor, whizz the flour and butter together briefly to create a breadcrumb texture. Add the egg and a splash of cold water to bind. As soon as the pastry starts to come together, stop whizzing and bring it together with your hands. Wrap in cling film (plastic wrap) and chill in the fridge for at least 30 minutes.

Lightly flour a work surface and roll out the pastry to a 2–3mm (1/16in) thickness. Lay the pastry over the floured rolling pin and carefully place into the tart ring, pushing it down to form the base, and leaving a little overhang of pastry over the side. It may look shabby now, but this can be trimmed off afterwards.

Chill the tart ring on the baking tray for another 20 minutes in the fridge.

Preheat the oven to 210°C/190°C fan/415°F/gas mark 6–7.

When ready to cook the tart, scrunch up some baking paper, flatten it out again, lay the paper on top of the pastry in the tart tin and fill with ceramic baking beans.

Cook in the oven for about 20 minutes until the sides and the base are cooked. Remove the baking paper and the beans. Turn the oven down to 170°C/150°C fan/325°F/gas mark 3.

For the filling, whisk the eggs with the cream and milk in a large bowl and season with salt and pepper.

Heat a large pan and add the butter. Once melted, cook the spinach for a few minutes until soft and wilted. Lightly grate some fresh nutmeg over the top of the cooked spinach and transfer to a colander lined with muslin (cheesecloth) to drain. Gently squeeze with your hands to remove as much excess water as you can.

Scatter the cooked spinach over the base of the cooked tart shell, sprinkle half the cheese over the top, then pour in the egg mixture, up to the top of the pastry shell. Tip: before adding the egg mixture, place the tart shell on the baking tray onto the oven shelf, and then add the liquid. Finally, sprinkle over the remaining cheese.

Bake in the oven for around 30 minutes, checking after 20 minutes. You want the very centre of the tart to still have a slight wobble when you take it out. Keep checking every 5 minutes or so to get it right. As soon as you have removed the tart from the oven, grate a fine layer of nutmeg over the top of the tart, so that it sticks while warm.

Leave to cool. This is best served warm or at room temperature but never straight from the fridge.

PUGLIAN STUFFED AUBERGINE WITH OREGANO AND PINE NUTS

Serves 4

This is a southern Italian dish, very typical of the region. Over the years I've spent many happy holidays in and around Puglia, and great seasonal vegetables are the order of the day. I recently had something very similar to this, only they were baby aubergines, served as part of a large selection of grazing plates – which, to my mind, is the best way to enjoy this type of regional dish.

2 large aubergines (eggplants), halved lengthways
5 tbsp good olive oil, plus extra for drizzling
½ onion, chopped
2 garlic cloves, finely chopped
1 celery stick, chopped
½ fennel bulb, cored and chopped
200g (7oz) spicy pork sausage, fennel ideally, skin removed and crumbled by hand
25g (1oz) fresh white breadcrumbs
4 tbsp pine nuts
20g (1oz) baby capers, drained
1 medium free-range egg, beaten
1 tbsp dried oregano
50g (1¾oz) Parmesan or pecorino, grated
6 sun-dried tomatoes, chopped
2 tbsp chopped oregano
Sea salt and freshly ground black pepper

Preheat the oven to 200°C/180°C fan/400°F/gas mark 6.

Using a small sharp knife, cut all around the aubergine (eggplant) halves, about 2cm (¾in) from the edges, and scoop out the flesh. You will have four hollowed-out aubergine shells. Roughly chop the flesh and set aside.

Heat a large frying pan (skillet) and add 3 tablespoons of the oil. Once hot, add the onion, garlic, celery and fennel. Season with salt and pepper and cook, stirring, until soft.

Add the crumbled sausage and cook for 10 minutes. Add the aubergine flesh and breadcrumbs to the pan, give it a stir, then add the pine nuts and cook, stirring, for a further 5–8 minutes.

Transfer this mixture to a bowl and add the capers, egg, oregano and cheese. Season with salt and pepper and mix well.

Stuff the aubergines with the cooked sausage mixture and place them in a deep baking tray. Drizzle liberally with olive oil and pour in enough water to form a 2cm (¾in) layer in the bottom of the tray, to steam and soften the aubergine as it cooks. Cover with foil and bake in the oven for 40 minutes, then remove the foil and cook for another 10 minutes.

Mix the sun-dried tomatoes with the fresh oregano and add just enough of the remaining 2 tablespoons of olive oil to bind.

Serve the baked aubergines on warmed plates, with the sun-dried tomato mixture spooned over the top.

GARDEN SALAD WITH GOAT'S CHEESE
AND CROUTONS

Serves 2 as
a starter or 4 as
a side dish

For the salad
150g (5½oz) sugar snap peas
300g (10½oz) young peas, fresh
  from the pod (podded weight)
150g (5½oz) assorted salad
  leaves; use whatever
  is in season
½ bunch of chives, finely
  chopped
40g (1½oz) pea shoots
10–12 mint leaves
Sea salt and freshly ground
  black pepper
100g (3½oz) baked or fried
  croutons, to serve

**For the dressing and
goat's cheese**
1 banana shallot, chopped
2–3 tbsp balsamic vinegar
1–2 tsp runny honey
5 tbsp olive oil
150g (5½oz) soft mild
  goat's cheese
60g (2¼oz) crème fraîche
1 tsp chopped thyme leaves

**Fresh and vibrant, this is a classic spring or summer salad.
Choose a soft, mild goat's cheese – otherwise the flavour
will overpower the freshness of the vegetables.**

Blanch the sugar snaps and the peas in boiling salted water
for no more than 1 minute, just to take the edge off the
rawness, then refresh them in ice-cold water for 1–2 minutes
to cool. Drain and reserve.

To make the dressing, mix the shallot in a bowl with the
vinegar and honey, then whisk in the oil. Season with salt
and pepper and set aside.

Using a fork, mash the goat's cheese in a separate
bowl until smooth. Add the crème fraîche and mix well,
adding the chopped thyme leaves. Taste and season with
salt and pepper.

Dollop the goat's cheese mixture into a serving dish,
spreading it out with the back of a spoon over the base
of the dish.

Toss the salad leaves with the chives, pea shoots, mint
leaves, sugar snaps and peas, and arrange on top of the
goat's cheese mix. Scatter over the croutons and drizzle
over the dressing to serve.

ROAST BUTTERNUT SQUASH WITH PANCETTA AND GRUYÈRE AND PARMESAN CREAM

Serves 2

A rather decadent way to dress up a butternut squash. Bacon or pancetta and cheese seem to be regulars in my recipes, and I'm unapologetic on this point – they do make everything taste better!

2 tbsp olive oil
4 slices of pancetta
1 butternut squash, peeled
   and sliced into 3–5cm
   (1–2in) thick pieces
1 rosemary sprig
1 garlic clove, finely chopped
300ml (10½fl oz) double
   (heavy) cream
100g (3½oz) Parmesan, grated
100g (3½oz) Gruyère
   cheese, grated
Sea salt and freshly ground
   black pepper

For the kale vinaigrette
50g (1¾oz) kale, trimmed and
   very finely chopped
2 tbsp red wine vinegar
3 tbsp olive oil
1 banana shallot, sliced into
   thin rounds

Heat the olive oil in a large pan over a medium heat and cook the pancetta for a few minutes to release the fat. Remove the pancetta from the pan and set aside. Add the squash, rosemary and garlic, to the pan with the pancetta fat, season with salt and pepper and cook for 20 minutes, stirring from time to time to make sure it's not sticking. Set aside and keep warm.

Bring the cream to the boil in a pan, then immediately remove from the heat and whisk in both cheeses until melted and thickened. Keep warm.

For the kale vinaigrette, using your hands, scrunch the chopped kale with the red wine vinegar in a bowl. Leave for 5 minutes to soften, then add the olive oil and shallot and a pinch of salt and black pepper.

When you're ready to serve, pour some of the Gruyère and Parmesan cream into each bowl, spoon in some squash and garnish with the kale vinaigrette, with the pancetta crumbled over in shards.

ROASTED WINTER VEGETABLES WITH COMTÉ CHEESE AND BACON

Serves 2

4 slices of good-quality streaky
    bacon, smoked or unsmoked
1 rosemary sprig
1 banana shallot, quartered
½ small cauliflower, broken
    into small florets, along
    with the leaves
4 Brussels sprouts, trimmed
    and halved
½ small squash, peeled, seeds
    removed and chopped into
    1cm (½in) cubes
¼ celeriac, peeled and finely
    chopped into 1cm (½in) cubes
Sea salt and freshly ground
    black pepper
Bunch of watercress, separated
    into sprigs, to serve

For the croutons
1 tbsp olive oil
2 slices of sourdough, cut into
    1cm (½in) cubes

For the warm Comté cheese
300g (10½oz) Comté
    cheese, grated
2 tsp Dijon mustard
50ml (2fl oz) lager or pale ale
3 medium free-range egg
    yolks, beaten

Roasting the vegetables in the bacon fat before serving with the comforting melted cheese mixture makes this winter dish something quite special. Proper comfort food.

Preheat the oven to 200°C/180°C fan/400°F/gas mark 6.

Heat a medium frying pan (skillet) over a medium heat. When hot, add the bacon and rosemary and cook until the bacon crisps up nicely, then remove and set aside. Discard the rosemary from the pan but reserve the bacon fat.

Put all the vegetables, apart from the cauliflower leaves, on a baking tray, Pour the bacon fat over the vegetables, mix well and season with salt and pepper. Roast for about 20 minutes until the vegetables are soft. Add the cauliflower leaves to the tray for the last 5 minutes of cooking.

To make the croutons, heat a medium frying pan over a medium heat and add the olive oil. When hot, add the sourdough cubes and cook, stirring, for 2–3 minutes, or until crisp. Transfer to a plate lined with paper towels to drain.

Preheat a grill (broiler) to medium. Mix all the ingredients for the cheese mixture in a bowl, spoon into an ovenproof dish large enough to hold the roasted vegetables and grill (broil) until bubbling.

Remove the ovenproof dish from under the grill and scatter the croutons and the roasted vegetables over the molten cheese base.

Break the bacon into pieces and scatter on top of the vegetables along with the fresh watercress.

HOME-SALTED COD WITH CHORIZO AND SAFFRON AIOLI

Serves 2

20g (¾oz) flaked sea salt
500g (1lb 2oz) cod loin,
    pin-boned and skin on
5 tbsp olive oil
200g (7oz) chorizo, chopped into
    bite-size pieces
4 banana shallots, peeled
    and quartered
2 thyme sprigs
1 small fennel bulb, cored and
    thinly sliced
125ml (4fl oz) dry white wine
    or fino sherry
1 bunch of cavolo nero,
    roughly chopped

For the saffron aioli
1 small baking potato, skin on
3 large garlic cloves, peeled
    and made into a paste using
    ½ tsp sea salt
Pinch of saffron
1 large free-range egg yolk
300ml (10½fl oz) olive oil
Juice of 1 lemon

Home-salting is a great way to firm up a delicately fleshed fish like cod. It changes the texture, giving it a much denser, meatier taste. This, for me, is a nicer way to eat salt cod than the rock-hard stuff you might find in some European markets. You will need to salt the cod the day before.

Sprinkle half the sea salt over the base of a deep ceramic baking dish. Put the cod on top and sprinkle over the rest of the sea salt. Place another, slightly smaller, dish on top and weigh it down with several tins or jars. Transfer the fish to the fridge, covered, and leave overnight.

The next day, remove the fish from the dish and rinse well in cold running water. Pat dry.

Preheat the oven to 200°C/180°C fan/400°F/gas mark 6.

To make the saffron aioli, put the potato on a baking tray and cook in the oven for an hour, then remove and cool. Leave the oven on.

Once the potato has cooled, put it into a large pestle and mortar and add the pasted garlic, the saffron and egg yolk and mix well. Gradually drizzle in the olive oil, whisking continuously with the pestle, to form a sauce with the consistency of thick double (heavy) cream. Squeeze in the lemon juice, check the seasoning and set aside.

Heat a large ovenproof frying pan (skillet) over a medium-high heat and add 2 tablespoons of the olive oil. When hot, add the cod, flesh-side down, and cook for 4–5 minutes, or until a brown crust starts to form on the bottom. Transfer to the oven and cook for a further 6–8 minutes, depending on the thickness of the fish.

Heat a separate frying pan over a medium heat and the remaining olive oil. When hot, add the chorizo and fry until crisp, then stir in the shallots, thyme and fennel and cook for a few minutes, just to warm through. Add the wine or sherry and cook to reduce for a few minutes before adding the chopped cavolo nero to the pan and allowing it to wilt.

Pile up the chorizo mixture on a warmed serving platter, spoon over some of the aioli and top with the roasted cod. Serve the remaining aioli alongside for dipping.

Saturday Night

SQUID TOASTS WITH CUCUMBER PICKLE

Serves 4
as a starter or
6 as a snack

For the squid toasts

2cm (¾in) piece root ginger,
    peeled and chopped
2 red chillies, deseeded
    and chopped
2 garlic cloves, chopped
2 tbsp Thai fish sauce
1 medium free-range egg white
450g (1lb) baby squid with
    tentacles, cleaned, squid
    bodies and tentacles
    kept separate
1 tsp toasted sesame oil
2 tsp light soy sauce
2 spring onions (scallions),
    chopped
1–2 tsp cornflour (cornstarch),
    to bind the mix if necessary
Vegetable oil, for deep-frying
4 thick slices of white bread
40g (1½oz) black sesame seeds
Sea salt and freshly ground
    black pepper

For the cucumber pickle

1 tbsp vegetable oil
2 garlic cloves, finely chopped
50g (1¾oz) cashews, chopped
1 red chilli, deseeded
    and chopped
4 tbsp soy sauce
1 tbsp white wine vinegar
20g (¾oz) palm sugar
½ cucumber, coarsely grated,
    excess water squeezed out
2 tbsp chopped coriander
    (cilantro) leaves, to serve

A delicious alternative to the much-loved prawn (shrimp) toasts. It's so easy to make your own version and adjust the seasonings to suit your tastes.

Blitz the ginger, chillies, garlic, fish sauce and egg white in a food processor to combine. Add the squid bodies and pulse until the mixture has a smooth consistency. Add the sesame oil and light soy sauce and pulse briefly to combine. Season with salt and pepper and stir in the spring onions (scallions).

If the mixture looks too wet at this stage, add the cornflour (cornstarch). Chill the mixture in the fridge for 20–30 minutes to firm up.

To make the cucumber pickle, heat the oil in a frying pan over a medium heat, add the garlic, cashews and chilli and cook, stirring, until crisp, 2–3 minutes. Add the soy sauce, vinegar and palm sugar and cook, stirring, until the sugar has dissolved. Add the cucumber to the pan and stir for 1–2 minutes, then remove from the pan and set aside in a bowl to cool.

Heat the vegetable oil in a deep-fat fryer to 180°C (350°F). If you don't have a fryer, half-fill a deep, heavy-based pan with vegetable oil set over medium-high heat. The oil is hot enough when a small cube of bread dropped into the oil turns golden brown in 40–50 seconds (or you can test the temperature using a probe thermometer).

Spread the chilled squid toast mixture generously and evenly over the bread slices and sprinkle over the black sesame seeds.

Deep-fry the toasts in batches for 4–5 minutes until the bread is golden, using a slotted metal spoon to turn them over halfway through cooking. Remove the toasts and drain on a plate lined with paper towels. Keep them warm while you cook the rest. You can trim away the crusts now if desired.

While the toasts are draining, deep-fry the squid tentacles for 30–60 seconds, then remove and drain.

Serve the squid toasts on a serving plate with the cucumber pickle and the coriander (cilantro) leaves scattered over.

Saturday Night

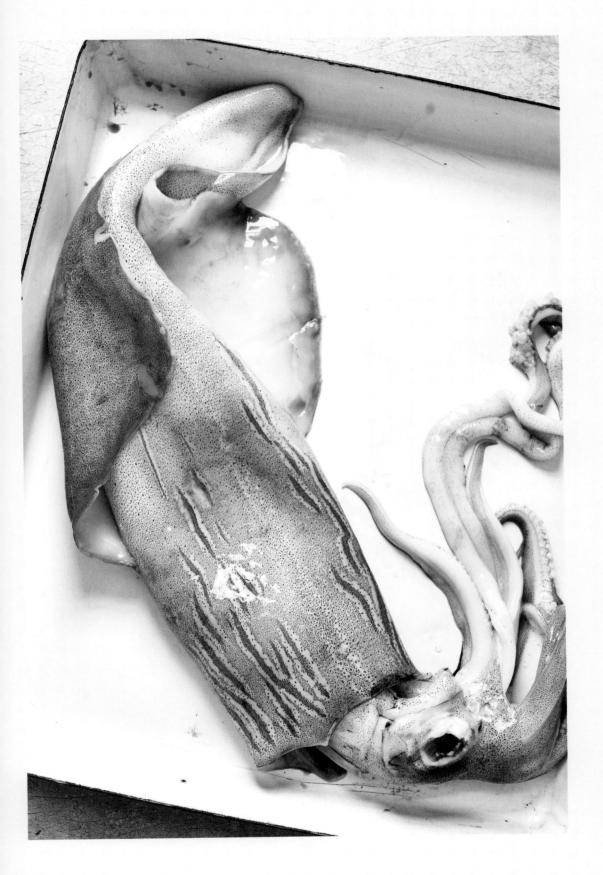

SAUTÉED CHILLI SQUID WITH SQUID INK SAUCE AND GREMOLATA

**Serves 2
as a starter**

1 small-medium squid, about
    120–150g (4¼–5½oz), cleaned
    and thinly sliced
1 tbsp vegetable oil
Juice of 1 lemon
1 red chilli, deseeded and
    finely chopped
1 garlic clove, finely chopped
200g (7oz) tinned chickpeas,
    drained
1 celery stick with its leaves,
    finely chopped
1 tbsp sherry vinegar
3 tbsp extra virgin olive oil
Sea salt and freshly ground
    black pepper

For the gremolata
1 garlic clove, finely chopped
Zest of 1 lemon
4 tbsp chopped flatleaf parsley

For the sauce
200ml (7fl oz) fish stock
3½ tbsp Noilly Prat or other
    dry white vermouth
2 small squid ink sachets
    (optional; available from
    fishmongers and some
    supermarkets)
1 banana shallot, finely chopped
3–4 tbsp olive oil
2 tbsp red wine vinegar

This is a show-off, 'I've-really-gone-to-town' Saturday night starter. If you can't get hold of the squid ink, it's still a great dish to make. The ink just adds another layer of flavour (and the black colour looks cool).

First heat a frying pan (skillet) until scorching hot. Toss the sliced squid in a bowl with the oil and season with salt and pepper. Toss the squid into the hot pan and cook, stirring, for 1 minute. Add the lemon juice, then remove the squid from the pan and transfer to a clean bowl. Add the remaining squid ingredients to the bowl and season again with salt and pepper.

Mix all the gremolata ingredients together in a small bowl and set aside.

To make the squid ink sauce, put the fish stock in a small pan over a high heat and cook until it is reduced by half, about 5 minutes. Add the Noilly Prat and cook over a high heat, again until reduced by half, about 5 minutes. Add the ink sachets, if using, and cook for a few minutes more. The sauce should have the consistency of single (light) cream.

Put the chopped shallots in a bowl, pour the sauce over the shallots then mix in the oil and vinegar. Taste and season with salt and pepper. Leave to cool.

When you're ready to serve, spoon the squid ink sauce into a serving bowl. Pile the chickpeas and squid on top and garnish with the gremolata.

KING SCALLOPS WITH PICKLED GIROLLES AND SEAWEED BUTTER

Serves 2

100ml (3½fl oz) water
100ml (3½fl oz) malt vinegar
150g (5½oz) girolle or chanterelle
    mushrooms, brushed clean
4 tbsp olive oil
2 fresh corn on the cob,
    kernels removed
2 spring onions (scallions),
    chopped
6 fat king (sea) scallops with roe
Sea salt and freshly ground
    black pepper

For the seaweed butter
100g (3½oz) unsalted butter,
    softened and kept at room
    temperature
1–2 tbsp dried seaweed, such as
    nori or dulse, crumbled
1 heaped tbsp white miso paste

This makes a special starter, ideally around late summer when both sweetcorn (corn) and girolles are in season. Don't be put off by the thought of seaweed butter. It's there to supercharge the taste of the scallops by adding another layer of that all-important savoury umami flavour.

You can make the seaweed butter in advance: put all the ingredients in a bowl and mix well. Taste and season with salt and pepper. Set aside.

Bring the water and vinegar to the boil in a saucepan over a high heat and bubble until the liquid is reduced by half, 2–3 minutes. Take off the heat, add the mushrooms and set aside to marinate for 1 hour.

Meanwhile, heat half the oil in a pan over a high heat and, when hot, add the corn kernels and cook, stirring, until soft (no more than 1–2 minutes). Remove the pan from the heat and add the spring onions (scallions) and 1–2 tablespoons of the seaweed butter. (Leftover butter will keep in the fridge for 3–5 days or wrapped in the freezer for 3 months.)

Season the scallops with salt and pepper. Heat a dry frying pan (skillet) over a high heat until smoking hot, then add the remaining oil and the seasoned scallops. Cook on one side until golden brown (no more than 2 minutes), carefully turn the scallops over and remove the pan from the heat, allowing the scallops to rest in the pan.

Spoon the cooked corn and spring onions into a serving dish, scatter over the marinated mushrooms, then top with the scallops. I like to drizzle the scallops with some melted seaweed butter before serving.

SEA BASS WOK FISH

Serves 4

For the aubergines and mushrooms
2 tbsp vegetable oil
1 aubergine (eggplant), chopped
100g (3½oz) shiitake mushrooms,
    roughly chopped
100g (3½oz) oyster mushrooms,
    roughly chopped
Sea salt and freshly ground
    black pepper

For the garnish
1 red chilli, deseeded and finely
    chopped
100g (3½oz) cashews, toasted in
    a dry pan and roughly chopped
½ bunch of coriander (cilantro),
    leaves picked
½ bunch of mint, leaves picked
2 spring onions (scallions), chopped

For the sea bass
Vegetable oil, for deep-frying
1kg (2lb 4oz) sea bass, skin deeply
    scored down to the bone using
    the tip of a sharp knife at
    regular intervals along the
    length of the fish
50g (1¾oz) cornflour (cornstarch),
    seasoned with sea salt and
    freshly ground black pepper
2 limes, for squeezing, to serve

For the dressing
2 tbsp Thai fish sauce
3 tbsp palm sugar
2 garlic cloves, finely chopped
2cm (¾in) piece root ginger,
    peeled and finely chopped
3 lime leaves, shredded
2 lemongrass sticks, outer leaves
    removed, core finely chopped
3 tbsp rice wine vinegar
2 tbsp soy sauce
2 tbsp Chinese rice wine

One of my first kitchen jobs was in a fantastic restaurant called Vong, in Knightsbridge, London. It was owned by the famous chef Jean-Georges Vongerichten, whose food drew on French and Asian influences. One night I was lucky enough to be shown how to cook a dish called wok fish. It was essentially a whole deep-fried red snapper, which was plunged into boiling oil for a few minutes to crisp up, then dressed at the table in front of the diners with an aromatic, spicy oil. That was around 25 years ago, but I still remember how impressive it looked and how wonderful the aromas were. This is my version.

For the aubergines (eggplant) and mushrooms, heat the oil in a frying pan. When hot, add the aubergines and mushrooms and stir-fry until soft, 6–8 minutes. Season with salt and pepper to taste, cover and keep warm.

To make the garnish, mix the chilli with the toasted, chopped cashews and spring onions (scallions) in a bowl and toss with the fresh herbs. Set aside.

Next, fill a large wok (or deep-fat fryer) two-thirds full with vegetable oil. Heat over a medium-high heat until the oil reaches 180°C (350°F). The oil is hot enough when a small cube of bread dropped into the oil turns golden brown in 40–50 seconds (or you can test the temperature using a probe thermometer). Dredge the sea bass in the seasoned cornflour and deep-fry for 7–8 minutes. Make sure it's cooked through to the bone by testing it with the tip of a sharp knife – the flesh will easily come away from the bone when it is cooked and the fish should look crisp and golden.

While the fish is frying, heat all the ingredients for the dressing in a small pan over a medium heat, stirring to meld the flavours and dissolve the sugar.

Serve the sea bass on a warmed serving platter with the aubergine and mushrooms alongside. Pour the warm dressing over the top and scatter over the garnish. Serve with the lime wedges.

ROAST BASS WITH FENNEL AND LEMON THYME

Serves 2

Cooking this highly prized fish whole makes for a real celebration dish, and it looks great served in the centre of the table ready for sharing. With its firm white flesh, sea bass is also the perfect fish to roast with fragrant lemon thyme.

1 x whole sea bass, minimum
    1kg (2lb 4oz), cleaned,
    scaled and gutted
2 tbsp olive oil
500g (1lb 2oz) potatoes, peeled
    (use a waxy variety)
4 whole garlic cloves
1 bunch of lemon thyme
2 bay leaves
1 lemon, sliced
1 fennel bulb, trimmed and cut
    into 8–12 pieces
3 tbsp small capers, drained
3½ tbsp olive oil
150ml (5fl oz) dry white wine
Sea salt and freshly ground
    black pepper

For the salad
1 red chicory (endive),
    leaves separated
1 yellow chicory (endive),
    leaves separated
Large handful of watercress
Extra virgin olive oil
Juice of 1 lemon

Preheat the oven to 220°C/200°C fan/425°F/gas mark 7.

Pat the fish dry with paper towels and use the tip of a sharp knife to crisscross the flesh at regular intervals on both sides. Season the bass with sea salt and rub with the olive oil.

Put the potatoes and the garlic into a large pan of cold salted water over a high heat and bring to the boil. Turn the heat down and simmer until the potatoes are just tender when tested with the tip of a sharp knife. Drain and, when cool enough to handle, cut into 1cm (½in) thick slices. Reserve the garlic cloves.

Stuff the cavity of the fish with half the lemon thyme, the bay leaves and a few lemon slices.

Arrange the sliced potatoes and fennel in the base of a baking tray with the reserved garlic cloves and the capers. Lay the fish on top and drizzle the whole dish with the olive oil. Pour in the wine and scatter over the rest of the lemon thyme and the remaining lemon slices. Roast for 25–30 minutes until cooked through. The fish is cooked when the flesh easily pulls away from the bone when tested with the tip of a sharp knife.

For the salad, in a large bowl, combine the two types of chicory leaves and the watercress. Dress with the extra virgin olive oil and lemon juice.

Arrange the roasted potatoes, fennel and lemon slices on a warmed serving platter. Carefully lift the flesh from the bone and lay it over the potatoes. Grind over some black pepper and serve with any cooking juices from the baking tray, with the chicory salad alongside.

Serves 6

This needs some focused effort before you can sit back and enjoy it, but then it's just a case of putting it altogether and making it look good. It's a great recipe for outdoor entertaining as the yoghurt and the marinade really hold onto their flavours cooked on an open grill. Use blood oranges for the salad when in season.

4 tbsp full-fat Greek yoghurt
4 tbsp harissa
Juice of 1 lemon
600g (1lb 5oz) monkfish fillets
Sea salt and freshly ground
    black pepper

For the flatbread

350g (12oz) plain (all-purpose)
    flour, plus extra for dusting
300ml (10½fl oz) warm water
1 tsp salt
7g (2¼ tsp) fast-action yeast
Pinch of sugar
120ml (4fl oz) full-fat Greek yoghurt
1 tbsp olive oil

For the salad

1 pomegranate, seeds removed
½ bunch of mint, leaves picked
½ bunch of coriander (cilantro),
    leaves picked
2 oranges, segmented, juice reserved
2 tsp sumac, or to taste
2 tbsp pomegranate molasses
3 tbsp olive oil

For the za'atar

1 tsp white sesame seeds,
    toasted in a dry pan
1 tsp black sesame seeds,
    toasted in a dry pan
2 tsp dried oregano
2 tsp dried marjoram
2 tsp sumac
1 tsp sea salt
2 tsp ground cumin
4 tbsp extra virgin olive oil

Mix the yoghurt, harissa and lemon juice together in a bowl and season with salt and pepper. Place the monkfish onto a baking tray. Spread the marinade over the fish, cover and refrigerate for a few hours.

For the flatbread, mix the flour, water, salt, yeast and sugar in a large bowl. Add the yoghurt and olive oil and mix to form a dough. You can do this by hand using a wooden spoon or in the bowl of a stand mixer fitted with a dough hook attachment. Knead for 15 minutes until the dough is smooth and elastic. Cover well, so a skin isn't formed, and leave to rise in a warm place until doubled in size, about 1 hour.

Divide the dough into 6 even balls approximately the size of a tennis ball, dust the work surface with flour, then use a rolling pin to roll the dough into even circles about the size of a small side plate or saucer.

Heat a large frying pan (skillet) over a high heat and cook the flatbreads in batches, until blistered on both sides. Wrap up the flatbreads and keep warm.

Preheat the oven to 240°C/220°C fan/475°F/gas mark 8.

Bring the monkfish fillets up to room temperature and then cook in the baking tray in the oven for 8–10 minutes, depending upon the size. To check if it's cooked, insert a wooden skewer into the thickest part. If there's little resistance, it's cooked. Set aside, covered, to rest.

While the monkfish is resting, mix all the salad ingredients together in a bowl. Put all the za'atar ingredients in a bowl with the olive oil and mix well to form a loose paste.

To serve, spread some of the za'atar mixture over the flatbreads. Scatter the salad over the flatbreads then slice the monkfish and arrange over the top.

Saturday Night

ROAST CHICKEN WITH SALT-AND-VINEGAR POTATO CHIPS AND BROWNED BUTTER BÉARNAISE

Serves 4

This is a take on chicken and chips using two different cooking methods, and adding some brown butter béarnaise sauce for good measure. Braising the legs with herbs and the fruity vermouth and garlic brings a delicious contrast to the simply roasted breast meat.

Buy a good free-range bird, not just for animal welfare concerns, but also for the better taste and texture you will get from a higher-quality bird. The salt and vinegar seasoning needs to be made the day before and makes more than you will need for this recipe, but you can store the leftover seasoning in a sealed jar for up to 3 months. If you want to get more creative, Jerusalem artichokes also make great chips.

For the salt and vinegar seasoning
3 tbsp fine salt
2 tbsp malt vinegar
½ tbsp cornflour (cornstarch)

For the chicken
1 x large (1.5–2kg/3½–4½lb) chicken, cut down into 1 crown and 2 legs (see below)
Sea salt and freshly ground black pepper

For the braised chicken legs
2 whole chicken legs
20 garlic cloves, peeled and left whole
1 tarragon sprig (from the bunch below)
1 parsley sprig
2 bay leaves
150ml (5fl oz) dry white vermouth or white wine
300ml (10½fl oz) water
Pinch of freshly grated nutmeg
6 celery sticks, roughly chopped
2 tbsp olive oil

Make the salt and vinegar seasoning the day before. Mix the salt, vinegar and cornflour (cornstarch) together in a small bowl. Spoon in a thin layer onto a piece of baking paper and leave overnight, uncovered at room temperature, to harden. The next day, crush to a fine powder and store in a jar at room temperature.

To prepare the chicken, gently push down on the backbone of the chicken to flatten a little and loosen up the joints. Hold one of the wings and bend it back. Using a sharp knife, cut the skin and tendons along the wing bone; do this to both wings until the wing is separated. Bend the thighs and legs backwards to pop the joint. Then slice the skin connected to the meat and bone. Now gently pull the leg from the bones; be careful as you don't want to lose the oyster that's attached. Turn the leg over so you can see the bone connecting the thigh and leg and, using your sharp knife, cut straight through so the leg and thigh are separate. Do this on both sides. Locate the centre breastbone and run your knife along the side of the bone from the top to the bottom of the breast until it is separated and removed. Do this on both sides. (Don't throw the bones away as they make great stock.)

Preheat the oven to 160°C/140°C fan/320°F/gas mark 3.

Weekend

Continued overleaf

For the roast chicken crown
1 chicken crown
100g (3½oz) butter, softened
2–3 tbsp chopped parsley
1 tarragon sprig (from the
    bunch below), leaves
    removed and chopped
Sea salt and freshly ground
    black pepper

For the chips
8 baby new potatoes (use a waxy
    variety), scrubbed but skin
    left on
Vegetable oil, for deep-frying

For the béarnaise sauce
250g (9oz) butter
150ml (5fl oz) dry white wine
1 banana shallot, chopped
3 white peppercorns
3 medium free-range egg yolks
1 bunch of tarragon, chopped
Juice of 1 lemon

Season the chicken legs well with salt and pepper. Put them in a lidded ovenproof casserole with all the braising ingredients. Cook, lid on, in the oven for 1½ hours, ensuring that the legs are cooked through (the juices will run clear when pierced with a skewer in the thickest part of the thigh).

To prepare the roast chicken crown, spread a little of the butter all over the breasts, carefully separating the skin from the flesh and smearing some butter under the skin. Season the skin with salt and pepper. Stuff the remaining butter and the herbs inside the chicken cavity.

When the chicken legs have been cooking for about 50 minutes, put the chicken crown in a roasting tin and cook in the oven for about 40 minutes, or until cooked through. At the end of cooking time, set aside to rest for at least 20 minutes (there is no need to rest the legs).

While the chicken is cooking, make the chips. Cut the potatoes lengthways into thin slices about 1mm thick (a mandoline is best for this). Drop the slices into a bowl of cold water to remove the excess starch and leave to soak for 10 minutes. Drain, then put the slices on a baking tray lined with paper towels and pat them dry.

To fry the chips, use a deep-fat fryer set at 180°C (350°F), or half-fill a deep, heavy-based pan with vegetable oil set over a medium-high heat. The oil is hot enough when a small cube of bread dropped into the oil turns golden brown in 40–50 seconds (or you can test the temperature using a probe thermometer).

Deep-fry the chips in batches until golden. Remove using a slotted spoon and drain on a baking tray lined with paper towels. Sprinkle the chips with the salt and vinegar seasoning and keep somewhere warm until ready to serve.

To make the béarnaise sauce, heat the butter in a small pan over a medium-high heat until the butter turns hazelnut brown and begins to smell nutty. Keep swirling the pan as the butter cooks to prevent burning. Set the browned butter aside to reach room temperature but don't let it harden.

In a separate small pan over a medium-high heat, heat the wine with the shallot and peppercorns for 2–3 minutes. Transfer to a food processor then add the egg yolks, tarragon and lemon juice and whizz together. Slowly pour in the browned butter, whizzing between additions, until the sauce thickens and has a silky texture.

To serve, split the crown down the middle into two breasts, cut the legs into thighs and drumsticks, and arrange on a warmed serving platter, with the potato chips and the béarnaise sauce on the side.

POT-ROASTED VEAL WITH WHITE CABBAGE AND CARAWAY

Serves 6

It is now possible to buy ethically produced veal, raised with the high welfare standards that we have come to expect. It's also worth noting that veal is a by-product of the dairy industry, so if we drink milk quite happily, then we need to support farmers and eat more veal.

If you can't get hold of veal breast, then any slow-cook cut, such as beef shin or rump, will work in this dish.

2kg (4lb 8oz) boneless rose veal breast
4 tbsp olive oil
50g (1¾oz) salted butter, softened
4 onions, sliced
½ bunch of thyme, left whole and tied with string
2 bay leaves
1 head of garlic, broken into cloves, skin removed
175ml (5½fl oz) dry white wine
225ml (7¾fl oz) beef stock
Sea salt and freshly ground blackpepper

For the cabbage and caraway
1 small white cabbage, cored and finely shredded
50g (1¾oz) butter
150g (5½oz) pancetta, chopped
2 garlic cloves, finely chopped
1 onion, thinly sliced
1 tbsp caraway seeds
150ml (5fl oz) white wine or cider vinegar
1 tbsp finely chopped flatleaf parsley
½ tbsp chopped tarragon

Preheat the oven to 180°C/160°C fan/350°F/gas mark 4. Season the veal breast with salt and pepper.

Heat an ovenproof casserole (use one with a lid) over a high heat and add the oil. Once hot, add the veal breast and sear on both sides until golden.

Spread the veal with the softened butter, throw in the onions, herbs and garlic and pour over the white wine. Turn the heat down to medium and cook, stirring, until the liquid is reduced by half, 10–15 minutes. Add the stock, put the lid on top and cook in the oven for 1½–2 hours.

At the end of the veal's cooking time, strain the liquid from the casserole into a medium saucepan. (Keep the veal warm.) Cook over a high heat until the liquid has reduced by one-third, 10–20 minutes. Taste and season.

While the cooking liquid is reducing, prepare the cabbage by blanching it in a large pan of lightly salted boiling water for 2–3 minutes until soft. Drain and set aside.

Heat a large frying pan (skillet) over a medium heat and add the butter. Once melted add the pancetta, garlic and onion and cook, stirring, until soft, about 10 minutes.

Throw in the caraway seeds and mix in the cabbage. Pour in the vinegar then cook, stirring, until the liquid is reduced by half. Stir in the parsley and tarragon then taste and season if necessary.

To serve, thinly slice the veal breast and place onto serving plates with the cabbage alongside. Spoon over the reduced cooking juices.

Saturday Night

CHICKEN, HAM HOCK AND JERUSALEM ARTICHOKE PITHIVIER

Serves 4

2 x 250g (9oz) chicken legs,
poached, cooled, meat
shredded into large,
chunky pieces

150g (5½oz) ham hock, poached,
cooled, meat chopped into 1cm
(½in) chunks (reserve a ladle
or two of the cooking liquor)

1 tsp chopped tarragon
1 tsp chopped chervil
1 tsp chopped chives
2 tsp chopped parsley
1 banana shallot, finely chopped
4 peeled and cooked Jerusalem
artichokes, roughly chopped
1 garlic clove, crushed
3 large outer leaves from
a Savoy dark green cabbage,
blanched and refreshed

1 x 500g (1lb 2oz) pack puff pastry,
divided in two, bottom half
rolled out into a 15cm (6in)
diameter circle and top
half rolled out into a 20–25cm
(8–10in) diamater circle

1 medium free-range egg, beaten

Salt and freshly ground
black pepper

For the mustard cream sauce
150ml (5fl oz) chicken stock
150ml (5fl oz) double
(heavy) cream
1 tsp Dijon mustard
1 tsp wholegrain mustard
2 tsp white wine vinegar

This pithivier, which is essentially a puff-pastry pie, does require a bit of time and effort but is a real showstopper when served.

Start by putting the chicken, ham, herbs and shallot in a bowl. Season with salt and pepper, add the Jerusalem artichokes and garlic and mix well. Add a spoonful or two of the ham cooking liquor to loosen it to a spoonable consistency.

Lay the blanched cabbage leaves out into a large round on a sheet of cling film (plastic wrap) large enough to hold the leaves with some space to spare. Spoon the filling on top of the leaves, then pull up the sides of the cling film to enclose the leaves and filling, forming a tight ball.

Once you have formed this tight ball shape, remove the cling film and lay the stuffed cabbage leaves on top of one circle of puff pastry. Using a pastry brush, brush all around the edge of the base circle with the beaten egg. Top with the other pastry circle and gently push the edges together to seal. Using the tip of a sharp knife, lightly score a pattern in the top, starting from the centre and radiating outwards.

Brush the top of the pithivier with the remaining beaten egg. Transfer the pithivier to a baking sheet lined with baking paper, then chill in the fridge for at least 30 minutes.

Preheat the oven to 220°C/200°C fan/425°F/gas mark 7.

When the pithivier has chilled, transfer it, on the baking sheet, to the oven and bake for 20–25 minutes, or until the pastry is golden brown.

Meanwhile, to make the mustard cream sauce, bring the chicken stock to the boil in a saucepan and whisk in the cream and the two types of mustard. Season with salt and pepper and add the vinegar to taste.

Cut the pithivier into quarters and serve with the mustard cream sauce.

Saturday Night

RACK OF LAMB WITH CHARRED BROCCOLI, RICOTTA, GRILLED CHILLIES AND ANCHOVY

Serves 2

This is a great combination of flavours. I could eat ricotta all day, and a well-made one is like nothing else. Westcombe Dairy in Somerset, make a fantastic one, and it's well worth seeking out on their website. The sweetness of the lamb, the tempered heat from the grilled chillies and the creaminess of the ricotta – heaven on a plate.

You will need to drain the ricotta the day before.

1 x 8-bone lamb rack
1 rosemary sprig
10g (¼oz) butter
1 garlic clove, peeled, left whole and smashed
Sea salt and freshly ground black pepper

For the charred broccoli with ricotta, grilled chillies and anchovy
230g (8oz) purple sprouting broccoli (broccoli raab)
2 red finger chillies, grilled (broiled) on a high heat with the skin on until blackened
1 x 250g tub good-quality ricotta, drained for 24 hours over a colander lined with muslin (cheesecloth)
30g (1oz) top quality anchovies (Ortiz ones are brilliant), drained
2 tbsp olive oil

Preheat the oven to 220°C/200°C fan/425°F/gas mark 7.

Season the lamb rack well with just sea salt. Heat an ovenproof heavy-based frying pan (skillet) over a high heat. When hot, add the lamb rack and hold it fat-side down in the pan for about 10 minutes until the fat has turned golden brown. Turn the rack fat-side up, transfer to the oven and cook until pink, around 10 minutes.

Take the pan out of the oven and, while still hot, throw the rosemary, butter and smashed garlic clove into the pan and set aside to rest for 10 minutes. Keep the juices in the pan for serving.

While the lamb is in the oven, make the broccoli, ricotta, grilled chillies and anchovy. Heat a dry frying pan over a high heat. When hot, add the purple sprouting broccoli (broccoli raab) and put a heavy pan on top, letting the broccoli blister and char in the pan, turning occasionally. This will take around 5 minutes.

Carefully slip the tough skins from the blackened chilies and discard. Pull the flesh away from the seeds into long strands.

To serve, slice the lamb rack into 8 individual cutlets. Break up the ricotta into chunks and serve with the charred broccoli, topped with the chilli and the anchovy fillets. Pour over any meat juices, drizzle with the olive oil and serve immediately.

SLOW-COOKED LAMB NECK WITH CORIANDER DRESSING

Serves 4

I love lamb neck. It's a fantastic, flavourful cut of meat and is often overlooked despite being relatively cheap to buy. Here it is cooked in a very fragrant, light summer broth so don't be put off by the thought of a heavy, wintry style of braise. The coriander (cilantro) dressing is a favourite of mine, but I know it's not everyone's herb of choice. You can easily leave it out and increase the quantity of the other herbs.

2 tbsp olive oil
1kg (2lb 4oz) middle lamb neck,
    cut into 2cm (¾in) chunks
1 onion, finely chopped
3 celery sticks, finely chopped
2 carrots, finely chopped
1 leek, finely chopped
½ fennel bulb, finely chopped
750ml (26fl oz) bottle dry
    white wine
3 plum tomatoes on the vine,
    roughly chopped
8 small new potatoes, peeled and
    cut in half
1 bunch of asparagus, woody ends
    removed, cut into thirds
Salt and freshly ground
    black pepper

For the dressing
4 tbsp olive oil
1 bunch of coriander (cilantro),
    finely chopped
¼ bunch of parsley,
    finely chopped
¼ bunch of mint, finely chopped
1 tbsp baby capers, drained
2 shallots, finely chopped
2 garlic cloves, crushed
1–2 tbsp red wine vinegar

To cook the lamb, heat the 2 tablespoons of oil in a large ovenproof casserole (use one with a lid) over a medium heat. Brown the lamb on all sides (you may need to do this is in batches) then remove from the pan to a plate and set aside.

Turn the heat down to low, then add the onion, celery, carrots, leek and fennel to the casserole and cook until softened, about 20 minutes. Add the wine and tomatoes, then return the lamb to the pan. Cover and cook for 1½–2 hours, or until the lamb is tender.

Add the new potatoes about 20 minutes before the end of the cooking time and continue cooking for another 15 minutes. Throw in the asparagus just before the end of the cooking time to gently poach for a few minutes.

Put all the dressing ingredients into a food processor and blend to a pesto consistency.

Serve the lamb in deep bowls with the coriander dressing spooned on top.

BEEF AND ONION PIE WITH PARSLEY, TARRAGON AND GARLIC AND ANCHOVY SAUCE

Serves 4–6

This is a version of a simple yet stunning dish I have been making for some time. It's based on an old Elizabeth David recipe that uses copious amounts of butter to form the base of the sauce. The garlic sauce is best made fresh so it will be at its punchiest. I've stolen the pastry recipe from the fabulous Quality Chop House in London, as it's the best one I've ever made.

175g (6oz) unsalted butter, softened
1kg (2lb 4oz) piece rump steak, cut into 2.5cm (1in) steaks
6 onions, thinly sliced
2 bay leaves
1 tbsp finely chopped thyme leaves
6 garlic cloves, sliced
Sea salt and freshly ground black pepper

For the pastry
525g (1lb 2½oz) chilled butter, diced
380g (13½oz) plain (all-purpose) flour, plus extra for dusting
10g (¼oz) salt
175ml (5½fl oz) cold water
1 medium free-range egg, beaten

For the sauce
2 garlic cloves, chopped
2 tbsp red wine vinegar
6 tbsp olive oil
6 anchovy fillets
2 dried red chillies, soaked in warm water for 15 minutes, drained and chopped
¼ bunch of tarragon, finely chopped
½ bunch of flatleaf parsley, finely chopped

Preheat the oven to 180°C/160°C fan/350°F/gas mark 4.

Smear the inside of a lidded casserole with the 175g (6oz) butter. I know it's a lot but, trust me, it works!

Season the steaks with salt and pepper and lay them flat in the bottom of the casserole. Add the onions, bay leaves, thyme and garlic and place the lid on top. There is no need to add liquid, as the butter and the juices from the meat will provide all that's needed. Cook in the oven for 1½–2 hours, then remove from the oven and allow to cool.

Increase the oven temperature to 200°C/180°C fan/400°F/gas mark 6.

Meanwhile, make the pastry: put the diced butter, flour, and salt in a food processor and pulse, adding the water bit by bit, until it comes together as a dough (you may not need all the water). Wrap and chill in the fridge for 30 minutes.

For the sauce, put all the ingredients into the cleaned food processor and blend until smooth.

Once the meat is cooled, spoon it and the contents of the casserole into a pie dish and stir in the garlic sauce.

Lightly flour a work surface and roll out the pastry to a 3mm/⅛in thickness, slightly larger and about the shape of the pie dish. Cut off a thin strip a bit longer than the circumference of the pie dish and set aside.

Brush the rim of the pie dish with water and top the pie with the pastry. Trim off the excess pastry from around the sides. Press the reserved strip of pastry around the edge of the pie dish to seal it well, trimming as needed.

Brush the pastry all over with the beaten egg and cut a small slit in the centre to let the steam escape. Cook in the oven for 30 minutes until golden brown.

SPICED MARINATED LEG OF LAMB WITH WHITE BEANS AND MINT CHUTNEY

Serves 6–8

For the lamb
1 onion, halved
1 tbsp whole black peppercorns
1 head of garlic, cut in half
    horizontally, skin left on
4cm (1½in) piece root ginger, cut
    through lengthways, skin on
2 bay leaves
30g (1oz) sea salt
1 x 2–2.5kg (4lb 8oz–5lb 8oz) leg
    of lamb, bone in
Freshly ground black pepper

For the marinade
150g (5½oz) full-fat Greek yoghurt
2 tbsp cumin seeds
2 tbsp coriander seeds
1 tbsp fennel seeds
2 tbsp tomato purée (tomato paste)
2 tbsp harissa paste
Juice of 1 lemon
4 garlic cloves, finely chopped
2 tsp grated root ginger

For the beans
2 x 400g (14oz) tins cannellini
    beans, drained and rinsed
1 garlic clove, finely chopped
1 bunch of dill, chopped
½ bunch of parsley, chopped
100ml (3½fl oz) extra virgin olive oil
2 tbsp white wine vinegar

For the mint chutney
1 Thai green chilli
1 bunch of mint, chopped
½ bunch of coriander (cilantro),
    chopped, stalks included
2 garlic cloves, chopped
Juice of 1 lemon
¼ tsp sea salt
3–3½ tbsp vegetable or
    rapeseed (canola) oil

I love this take on roast lamb. It's a bit unusual, but the method of poaching and then fiercely roasting the lamb produces brilliant results. This idea came from an old tandoori cookbook I have, in which large pieces of meat are first poached, then marinated and finished in a tandoor oven. You'll never get the exact taste that a wood-fired tandoor will give, but not many of us have that luxury at home. Taste-wise, this comes pretty close.

Place all the ingredients for the lamb, apart from the lamb itself, in a large pan of water and bring to the boil over a high heat.

Once it has come to the boil, place the leg of lamb into the liquid, reduce the heat to low and simmer very gently for 30 minutes (don't let it boil). Remove the lamb from the poaching liquid and allow to cool. When cool, use a sharp knife to make several deep slashes into the meat.

Mix the marinade ingredients together in a bowl. Rub the mixture all over the meat, working it into the slashes. Marinate for 2–3 hours, covered, at room temperature.

Preheat the oven to 240°C/220°C fan/475°F/gas mark 8. Put the lamb in a roasting tray and roast in the oven for 20–30 minutes until blistered and well coloured. To get the meat properly blistered, you may need to cook it under a hot grill (broiler), turning frequently. It depends upon how hot your oven gets. Once the meat is well blistered, remove and rest for 20 minutes, covered.

Meanwhile, for the white beans, put the beans into a large bowl along with all the other ingredients. Mix well and taste and season with salt and pepper.

For the mint chutney, chop and deseed the Thai green chilli. Put all the ingredients into a food processor and pulse to a coarse paste. Set aside in a bowl.

Once the meat has rested, slice it and serve with the white beans and the mint chutney on the side.

GNOCCHI ALLA ROMANA WITH BONE MARROW AND SAUTÉED KIDNEYS

Serves 4

This is the sort of proper, rich, gutsy food found in many restaurants in Rome. This gnocchi recipe is very different from the one you may be familiar with. It's a much more homespun one that I personally think is easier to make and more comforting to eat. Marrowbones are quite easy to get hold of these days. Some supermarkets stock them, as do most good butchers.

For the gnocchi
570ml (20fl oz) full-fat (whole) milk
130g (4½oz) semolina flour
Pinch of freshly grated nutmeg
Pinch of sea salt
30g (1oz) unsalted butter, plus extra for greasing
100g (3½oz) Parmesan, grated
2 medium free-range egg yolks
Sea salt and freshly ground black pepper

For the bone marrow
25g (1oz) unsalted butter
1 garlic clove, crushed
2 banana shallots, finely chopped
1 split marrowbone, approximately 20cm (8in) long
2 tbsp finely chopped parsley
50g (1¾oz) fresh breadcrumbs

For the sautéed kidneys
25g (1oz) unsalted butter
500g (1lb 2oz) veal or lamb kidneys
1 garlic clove, crushed
2 thyme sprigs
3½ tbsp Madeira

For the salad
1 tbsp roughly chopped parsley
1 banana shallot, thinly sliced
1 tbsp baby capers, drained
1 tbsp red wine vinegar
2–3 tbsp olive oil

Preheat the oven to 200°C/180°C fan/400°F/gas mark 6. Grease a shallow baking tray with butter.

Bring the milk to the boil in a saucepan over a medium heat, sprinkle in the semolina flour and whisk continually until smooth. Season with the nutmeg and salt and whisk in the butter, half the Parmesan and the egg yolks.

Once all the ingredients are combined, pour the mixture into the greased baking tray and allow to cool.

Cut out rounds, using a 5cm (2in) cutter, and arrange in an ovenproof dish. Grate over the remaining Parmesan and bake for 20 minutes, or until the tops of the gnocchi are golden brown.

For the bone marrow, melt the butter in a small saucepan and add the garlic and shallots. Cook gently for 5 minutes until softened.

Remove the marrow from the bone and cut into small pieces, reserving the bone. Mix the marrow with the cooked shallot and garlic, chopped parsley and fresh breadcrumbs. Pile the mixture back into the bone cavity and cook in the oven for 15 minutes, or until golden brown.

Next, cook the kidneys: add the butter to a hot frying pan and, when foaming, add the kidneys, garlic and thyme and cook until the kidneys are golden brown on both sides, about 3 minutes on each side, being careful not to overcook them!

Add the Madeira while the pan is still hot and use a wooden spoon to scrape up any browned bits from the bottom of the pan. Remove the kidneys and set aside to rest, covered to keep warm.

Mix all the salad ingredients together in a bowl and season with salt and pepper.

Serve the baked gnocchi in the centre of the plate with the bone marrow and kidneys on top, with the salad alongside.

POACHED FILLET OF BEEF WITH HOLLANDAISE BEURRE NOISETTE

Serves 2

It is unusual to poach a fillet of beef, but if you are careful with it and don't boil the stock as the meat cooks, this gentle cooking method will give you great results. Just remember to brown the meat well before adding it to the stock; otherwise the colour will be lost in the poaching process. Browning the butter for the hollandaise delivers a deep, nutty sweetness that's so much nicer and more complex than the usual hollandaise.

400ml (14fl oz) tin beef consommé
225ml (7¾fl oz) rich, deep red wine
Bouquet garni made from 1 bay leaf, 2 thyme sprigs and 6cm (2½in) celery stick tied together with kitchen string
2 garlic cloves, peeled and left whole
2 tbsp olive oil
400g (14oz) fillet of beef
2 large floury potatoes, left whole, skin on
75g (2½oz) unsalted butter
Salt and freshly ground black pepper

For the vinaigrette
½ banana shallot, finely chopped
5 tbsp red wine
1 tbsp red wine vinegar
3½ tbsp olive oil
Juice of ½ lemon
½ tsp finely chopped chives
½ tsp finely chopped tarragon

For the hollandaise beurre noisette
250g (9oz) unsalted butter
3 medium free-range egg yolks
Juice of 1 lemon
1 tbsp Dijon mustard

Bring to the boil the beef consommé, red wine, bouquet garni and garlic in a saucepan (use a pan large enough to comfortably hold the beef fillet and poaching liquid). When the liquid begins to boil, turn the heat down so the liquid is just below simmering – there should be an occasional 'blip' at the surface but it should not bubble at all.

Meanwhile, heat the oil in a frying pan (skillet) over a high heat. When hot, add the beef fillet and sear the beef all over until well coloured. Transfer the beef from the frying pan into the pan with the consommé stock and poach very gently for 6–8 minutes (do not let the liquid boil). Remove the beef and set aside to rest, covered with foil.

Boil the potatoes in a pan of lightly salted water until just cooked but still firm when tested with the tip of a sharp knife. Drain, leave to cool, then cut into 1cm (½in) slices. Melt the butter in the cleaned pan that you used to sear the beef in over a medium heat. Add the potatoes to the pan and cook on both sides until golden, 10–15 minutes. Season with salt and pepper.

For the vinaigrette, put the shallot and red wine in a small saucepan and bring to the boil. Boil rapidly to reduce the liquid down to about 1 tablespoon and until the shallots have turned deep red. Put the rest of vinaigrette ingredients in a small heatproof bowl, then pour over the shallot reduction and whisk well to combine.

To make the hollandaise beurre noisette, put the butter into a cold pan. (Using a pan with a pale-coloured base will make it easier to judge the colour of the butter as it cooks.) Put the pan over a medium heat and keep the pan moving, constantly swirling the butter until it turns a light caramel colour, about 5 minutes. When the butter smells nutty, immediately pour it into a cool bowl to stop it cooking further. Set aside.

Briefly blitz the egg yolks, lemon juice and a splash of water in a food processor then slowly add the browned butter, bit by bit and whizzing between additions, as if you are making mayonnaise. When all the butter has been mixed in, the sauce should look thick and glossy. At this point stir in the mustard and season to taste with salt and pepper. Add a squeeze more lemon juice if necessary.

When you are ready to serve, toss the potatoes in the vinaigrette and layer them onto a warmed serving plate. Slice the beef thickly and arrange on top of the potatoes. Spoon over the hollandaise beurre noisette and serve with vegetables of your choice.

Everyone loves a good Sunday lunch. It's an event in itself, and the one time I feel the need to be a bit more traditional with my cooking. It's also a great time to celebrate fantastic British farmers and the world-class ingredients they produce.

If you want to push the boat out now and again, I'd recommend a big rib of beef, well-aged and with a good covering of yellow fat. Serve it with family-size Yorkshire puddings to be torn apart at the table and some simple vegetables as the support act. If you want something lighter and less time-consuming but just as comforting, try the Veal and Ricotta Meatballs on page 176 or the Provence-style Tart with Roasted Lamb on page 183.

Sunday doesn't have to all be about big cuts of meat, simple soups are a great way to kickstart a long lunch. Keep them punchy and flavourful. The velvety Courgette and Parmesan Soup on page 164 is one of my favourites. Or, why not share a large piece of great fish, such as the Sautéed Ray Wing on page 174.

I love food from all around the world, but this is Sunday lunch. It's there to remind you where you are in the world and what day of the week it is. Other than a Bloody Mary, the only thing I crave on a Sunday is a proper lunch.

Sunday Lunch

COURGETTE AND PARMESAN SOUP

Serves 4

Courgettes (zucchini) do need a bit of help on the flavour front, but with the addition of all the bolder ingredients used in this recipe, you can turn them into this delicious soup. It's the perfect way to use up a glut of these vegetables – they do shrink down when cooked. This soup is best eaten warm, rather than very hot.

3 tbsp extra virgin olive oil
3 garlic cloves, sliced
1 onion, sliced
1 green chilli, chopped
1 Parmesan rind (optional)
1kg (2lb 4oz) courgettes
 (zucchini), chopped into 1cm
 (½in) chunks
1 litre (35fl oz) chicken or
 vegetable stock
200ml (7fl oz) double
 (heavy) cream
100g (3½oz) Parmesan, grated
1 bunch of coriander
 (cilantro), chopped
Sea salt and freshly ground
 black pepper

To serve
2 tbsp olive oil
50g (3½oz) Parmesan, grated
180g (6¼oz) tortilla chips

Heat the olive oil in a large pan over a medium heat. Add the garlic and onion and cook gently over a low–medium heat for 10 minutes before adding the chilli, Parmesan rind, if using, and the chopped courgettes. Cook, stirring, for another 5 minutes before adding the stock. Simmer for 10 minutes.

Remove the Parmesan rind, if used, purée half the soup in a blender or food processor, then add it back into the pan with the chunky vegetables.

Pour in the double (heavy) cream and add the grated Parmesan and the coriander (cilantro). Taste and season accordingly with salt and pepper.

Pour the soup into individual bowls and garnish with a drizzle of olive oil and some more grated Parmesan before serving, with tortilla chips on the side.

MUSHROOM AND TARRAGON SOUP

Serves 4–6

1 tbsp olive oil
55g (2oz) unsalted butter
1 onion, sliced
2 garlic cloves, sliced
2 celery sticks, finely chopped
1 bunch of tarragon, leaves
    removed and chopped,
    stalks chopped
10 large portobello mushrooms,
    roughly chopped
1 litre (35fl oz) water, chicken
    or vegetable stock
200ml (7fl oz) double
    (heavy) cream
100–150ml (3½–5fl oz) full-fat
    (whole) milk
6 Paris brown or small chestnut
    mushrooms, sliced, to garnish
Sea salt and freshly ground
    black pepper

A great traditional starter to a full-on Sunday lunch. Large field or portobello mushrooms would be my top pick, packed so full of flavour that there's not much for a cook to add. You can make this with a variety of different mushrooms, but for depth, meatiness, and texture I'd always go with these types. When the season allows, sauté some mixed wild mushrooms to add as a garnish instead of the Paris brown or chestnut mushrooms.

Heat the olive oil and 25g (1oz) of the butter in a large saucepan over a medium heat. Add the onion, garlic, celery and tarragon stalks and cook gently, stirring, until cooked but not coloured, about 10 minutes.

Add the portobello mushrooms to the pan and continue to cook over a medium heat to extract all the flavour from the mushrooms. After 10 minutes add the water or stock and simmer for 20–30 minutes. Add the cream, bring back to the boil, taste, and season with salt and pepper.

Whizz the soup in a food processor or blender until smooth and strain through a fine sieve (strainer) if necessary. If it's too thick, loosen with a bit more milk or water.

Heat the remaining butter in a frying pan over a medium-high heat until foaming. Add the sliced Paris brown or chestnut mushrooms and cook, stirring until browned, then add the chopped tarragon leaves and stir through.

Ladle the soup into individual bowls and garnish with the sautéed mushrooms scattered over the top of each.

FRENCH ONION SOUP WITH GRUYÈRE AND HAM CROUTONS

Serves 4

30g (1oz) unsalted butter
2 tbsp olive oil
4 large white onions, thinly sliced
1 tsp chopped thyme leaves
2 garlic cloves, peeled
   and crushed
1 bay leaf
1 tbsp yeast extract
30g (1oz) plain (all-purpose) flour
1 litre (35fl oz) beef stock
Sea salt and freshly ground
   black pepper

For the croutons
10g (¼oz) unsalted butter
10g (¼oz) plain (all-purpose) flour
100ml (3½fl oz) full-fat
   (whole) milk
1000ml (3½fl oz) double
   (heavy) cream
150g (5½oz) Gruyère
   cheese, grated
Pinch of cayenne pepper
½ thin French stick (baguette),
   cut into 5mm (¼in) thin slices
2 tbsp Dijon mustard
2 tbsp mayonnaise
2 slices of Bayonne ham, torn
   into small pieces

The only way to improve on a traditional French onion soup would be to combine it with that other classic, croque monsieur. That's just what these Gruyère and ham croutons do, so here it is. You're welcome!

Heat the butter and oil in a large saucepan over a low-medium heat (use a saucepan with a lid). Add the onions, thyme, garlic and bay leaf and cook slowly, with the lid on, for 20–25 minutes until the onions are soft. Stir in the yeast extract and cook for a further minute.

Stir in the flour and whisk in the stock. Bring the stock to the boil and simmer for 5–10 minutes, taste and season with salt and pepper.

For the Gruyère and ham croutons, you'll need to make a cheesy béchamel sauce. Heat the butter in a medium-sized saucepan over a medium heat. Once melted, stir in the flour. Gradually whisk in the milk and the cream. Add half of the grated Gruyère cheese and whisk until melted. Season with salt, pepper and mix in the cayenne pepper. Allow the sauce to cool. Cut a circle of baking paper and place on top while the sauce is cooling to prevent a skin from forming.

Preheat a grill (broiler) to medium and lightly toast the sliced French stick (baguette) on both sides. Brush half the slices with Dijon mustard and spread on the mayonnaise.

Place the ham and some of the remaining grated cheese on top and then sandwich together with the remaining toasted bread. Spoon on the sauce and top with the remaining handful of grated Gruyère.

Place back under the grill, increase the heat to high and cook until the cheese is melted and golden.

To serve, warm the soup bowls. Ladle the onion soup into the bowls and serve with the toasted croutons in the bowl and alongside.

SPRING MINESTRONE SOUP WITH HARISSA TOAST

Serves 4

2 tbsp olive oil
1 onion, finely diced
1 celery stick, finely diced
1 small courgette (zucchini),
    finely diced
2 garlic cloves, finely chopped
1 Parmesan rind (optional)
2 rosemary sprigs, leaves
    finely chopped
2 spring onions (scallions), white
    and green parts separated
    andchopped
4 asparagus spears, tips removed
    and reserved
150g (5½oz) fresh or frozen broad
    beans, double podded
    (podded weight)
400g (14oz) tin cannellini beans,
    drained and rinsed
400g (14oz) tin borlotti beans,
    drained and rinsed
1 litre (35fl oz) vegetable stock
Sea salt and freshly ground
    black pepper
150g (5½oz) Parmesan, finely
    grated, to serve

For the harissa toast
4 tbsp harissa paste
2 slices of ciabatta, toasted
2 tbsp chopped flatleaf parsley

I like the spicy kick these harissa toasts give the dish. I like a bit of heat, and I often chop up some chillies and stir them into whatever I'm making!

Begin by heating the oil in a large saucepan and gently frying the onion, celery, courgette (zucchini), garlic, Parmesan rind (if using) and rosemary for 15 minutes over a medium heat. Throw in the spring onions (scallions) and the asparagus spears (but don't add the tips at this stage). Cook gently, stirring, for a further 10 minutes.

Now add the beans and cook for a further 5 minutes. Add the stock and bring back to the boil, then add the asparagus tips and turn off the heat. Allow to stand for 10 minutes before serving – you can taste the vegetables better when they're not so hot. Taste and season with salt and pepper.

To make the harissa toast, spread the harissa paste on the toasted ciabatta slices and sprinkle with the parsley.

Ladle the minestrone soup into warmed serving bowls and grate the Parmesan over the top. Serve with the harissa toast on the side.

CRISP-FRIED GOAT'S CHEESE WITH HERB LENTILS AND SPICED ROASTED APPLE

Serves 4

The spiced roasted apple enlivens and contrasts with the rich goat's cheese and lentils. Or maybe this is just another vehicle for molten cheese!

For the spiced roasted apple

2 Cox apples (or similar crisp eating apples), cored and cut into quarters
1 red onion, cut into rings
1 red chilli, chopped, seeds left in
2 tbsp pine nuts
2 thyme sprigs
2 tbsp olive oil

For the goat's cheese

100g (3½oz) plain (all-purpose) flour, seasoned with salt and pepper
2 medium free-range eggs, beaten
100g (3½oz) panko breadcrumbs
225g (8oz) goat's cheese log
Vegetable oil, for deep-frying

For the lentils

400g (14oz) cooked Puy lentils (cooked weight)
2 tbsp chopped flatleaf parsley
1 tbsp finely chopped chives
3 tbsp extra virgin olive oil
1 tbsp sherry vinegar
1 garlic clove, peeled and crushed
Sea salt and freshly ground black pepper

To serve

½ red chicory (endive), leaves separated
½ yellow chicory (endive), leaves separated
3 tbsp olive oil
1 tbsp sherry vinegar

Preheat the oven to 200°C/180°C fan/400°F/gas mark 6. Put the apples, onion, chilli, pine nuts and thyme sprigs in a roasting dish, drizzle over the olive oil and mix well. Cook in the oven for 15–20 minutes, or until softened.

Put the flour, beaten eggs and panko breadcrumbs in three separate shallow bowls. Dip the goat's cheese log first in the flour, then in the beaten egg and finally the breadcrumbs until well coated.

Put the coated goat's cheese log in the freezer for at least 15 minutes until firm.

Next, preheat the oil in a deep-fat fryer set at 180°C (350°F), or half-fill a large, deep, heavy-based pan with oil set over a medium-high heat. The oil is hot enough when a small cube of bread dropped into the oil turns golden brown in 40–50 seconds (or you can test the temperature using a probe thermometer).

Gently lower the whole goat's cheese into the deep-fat fryer using a slotted metal spoon and fry until golden. Remove using the slotted spoon and drain on a plate lined with paper towels. Allow to cool slightly.

For the lentils, put the cooked lentils in a large bowl and stir through the parsley and chives. In a separate bowl make the dressing by whisking the oil, vinegar and garlic until thickened, then season with salt and pepper and stir to combine. Dress the lentils before serving.

When you're ready to eat, mix the chicory (endive) leaves with the oil and sherry vinegar. Spoon the lentils into the base of a serving dish and top with the spiced roasted apple mixture. Slice the fried goat's cheese and place on top along with the dressed chicory leaves.

PARMESAN FRITTERS WITH ROQUEFORT SPINACH

Serves 4

Vegetable oil, for deep-frying
100ml (3½fl oz) full-fat
   (whole) milk
50g (1¾oz) unsalted butter
100ml (3½fl oz) water
125g (4½oz) plain
   (all-purpose) flour
1 tsp English mustard powder
2 medium free-range eggs
1 tsp chopped thyme leaves
280g (10oz) Parmesan, grated
200g (7oz) baby spinach
3½ tbsp crème fraîche
3½ tbsp double (heavy) cream
100g (3½oz) Roquefort cheese
Pinch of freshly grated nutmeg

I love cheese (especially blue cheese) and I love fritters. The End!

Preheat the oil in a deep-fat fryer to 180°C (350°F), or half-fill a deep, heavy-based pan with oil set over medium-high heat. The oil is hot enough when a small cube of bread dropped into the oil turns golden brown in 40–50 seconds (or you can test the temperature using a probe thermometer).

Put the milk, butter and water in a large saucepan and bring to the boil. As soon as it comes to the boil, add the flour and mustard and beat together with a wooden spoon or large whisk to make a thick paste.

Take off the heat and allow to cool slightly (if you don't cool it the mixture may split). Gradually beat in the eggs, thyme and 200g (7oz) of the grated Parmesan.

Use a dessertspoon to gently drop each fritter into the hot oil and cook until crisped up and golden. They will take 4–5 minutes in the fryer, turning frequently. Remove and drain on plate lined with paper towels and keep warm.

Next, heat a large saucepan over a medium heat. Add the spinach and cook until wilted down, then add the crème fraîche, cream and Roquefort cheese and cook until the cheese is melted. Finish with the freshly grated nutmeg.

To serve, layer the spinach and cheese mixture onto a serving plate, top with the yummy fritters and sprinkle over the remaining grated Parmesan.

Serves 2 as
a starter

For the crispy eggs

50g (1¾oz) plain (all-purpose)
flour, seasoned with salt
and pepper

2 medium free-range soft-boiled
eggs, peeled

1 medium free-range egg, beaten

125g (4½oz) panko breadcrumbs

Vegetable oil, for deep-frying

For the ham hock and pea purée

500g (1lb 2oz) frozen peas,
defrosted

200g (7oz) cooked ham hock,
shredded (keep the stock
the ham was cooked in, and
keep warm)

150g (5½oz) fresh peas, out of
their pods (podded weight)

50g (1¾oz) mange tout (snow
peas) or sugar snap peas,
left whole

30g (1oz) pea shoots

2 mint sprigs, leaves picked

25g (1oz) Parmesan, shaved using
a vegetable peeler

2 tbsp olive oil

Juice of ½ lemon

Sea salt and freshly ground
black pepper

A classic combination of peas, ham and mint is
supercharged with a crispy, deep-fried egg. A sexy
little summertime starter!

First, put the seasoned flour in a shallow bowl. Roll each
soft-boiled egg in the seasoned flour, then the beaten egg,
then finally the breadcrumbs.

Heat a deep-fat fryer set at 180°C (350°F). If you don't
have a deep-fat fryer, half-fill a deep, heavy-based pan
with vegetable oil set over a medium-high heat. The oil is
hot enough when a small cube of bread dropped into the
oil turns golden brown in 40–50 seconds (or you can test
the temperature using a probe thermometer). Deep-fry the
eggs for 3–4 minutes until golden. Remove using a slotted
spoon and drain on a plate lined with paper towels.

To make the pea purée, blitz the defrosted peas with
1–3 ladlefuls of the warm ham stock in a blender or food
processor – add it bit by bit and use just enough to make
a smooth purée. Push through a sieve (strainer) into a bowl
(discard the skins left behind). Taste and season with salt
and pepper.

Bring a pan of water to the boil, then plunge the fresh
peas and mange tout (snow peas) into the boiling water
for 30 seconds. Drain and refresh in cold water.

Toss the fresh peas, mange tout, shredded ham hock,
pea shoots, mint and Parmesan in a bowl. Add the olive
oil and a squeeze of lemon juice, mix again and check
the seasoning.

Spread the pea purée over the base of the serving
plates. Pile on the ham hock, pea shoots and mint mixture
and finish with a crispy egg.

SAUTÉED RAY WING WITH CLAM VINAIGRETTE

Serves 4

If you've never tried ray wing then you are seriously missing out. So many horror stories from the past refer to this sweet, magnificent fish as giving off an ammonia smell, but this is only found in fish that have been kept too long. Buy it fresh from a reliable supplier, cook it simply and it really is very special.

For the clam vinaigrette
2 tbsp balsamic vinegar
2 tbsp sherry vinegar
1 banana shallot, chopped
5 tbsp olive oil
½ bunch of chives, finely chopped
1kg (2lb 4oz) small fresh clams, rinsed, scrubbed and soaked in cold, clean water for a few hours (discard any open clams that don't shut when tapped on a hard surface)
100ml (3½fl oz) fino sherry

For the ray wing
1.5kg (3lb 5oz) ray wing, cut through the bone into 4cm (1½in) pieces
100g (3½oz) plain (all-purpose) flour, seasoned with salt and pepper
2 tbsp olive oil
15g (½oz) unsalted butter
2 tbsp sherry vinegar
Sea salt and freshly ground black pepper

Start by making the clam vinaigrette. Whisk both vinegars in a bowl with the shallot and olive oil. Taste, season with salt and pepper and stir in the chives. Set aside.

Heat a large shallow pan with a lid and add the clams and the fino sherry. Cover with the lid and shake the pan from time to time until all the clams are open (discard any clams that do not open).

Tip the clams into a colander lined with a piece of muslin set over a bowl to catch the cooking juices. Allow to cool before picking the meat from the shells and dropping into the reserved clam cooking juices. Add the vinaigrette to the cooking juices and set aside.

To prepare the ray wing, trim away and discard the thin end of the fish, to neaten it up. Put the seasoned flour on a plate and dip the ray pieces into it.

Heat a non-stick frying pan (skillet) over a high heat and add the olive oil. When hot, add the fish pieces thick-side down. Cook gently on this first side for around 5 minutes before turning over to the thinner side and cooking for a further 5 minutes.

Check the fish is cooked through by pushing a cocktail stick into it. If it goes in without much resistance, it's cooked. Add the butter and the sherry vinegar and baste the fish in these juices.

Serve the ray with a generous spoonful of the clam vinaigrette over the top.

VEAL AND RICOTTA MEATBALLS WITH TOMATO SAUCE

Serves 4

I was filming in New York some time ago and was very fortunate to be shown this meatball recipe by an Italian-American chef. Fortunate because it's simply the best meatball I've ever eaten. The surprising addition of ricotta gives soft, smooth, delicate results. If you can't get hold of veal mince (ground veal), then beef, pork or chicken also work well. Serve with spaghetti or pile into a baking dish and top with more ricotta and Parmesan, and bake until golden and oozing with bubbling cheese. That's my style!

For the tomato sauce
1 banana shallot, roughly chopped
2 garlic cloves, roughly chopped
1 red chilli, deseeded and
    roughly chopped
800g (1lb 12oz) ripe plum
    tomatoes, quartered
1 rosemary sprig, leaves
    roughly chopped
1 oregano sprig, leaves
    finely chopped
2 tbsp olive oil
200g (7oz) tomato passata
½ bunch of basil, leaves shredded
Sea salt and freshly ground
    black pepper

For the meatballs
250g (9oz) veal mince
    (ground veal)
100g (3½oz) Parmesan, grated
50g (1¾oz) pecorino, grated
1 tbsp finely chopped
    flatleaf parsley
250g (9oz) ricotta
½ medium free-range egg, beaten
4 tbsp olive oil

Preheat the oven to 200°C/180°C fan/400°F/gas mark 6.

Put the shallot, garlic, chilli, tomatoes, rosemary and oregano in a large roasting tin, season with salt and pepper and drizzle with the olive oil. Cook in the oven for 20–30 minutes, or until the tomatoes are soft and blistered – the colour is what gives the sauce its flavour.

While the sauce is cooking make the meatballs: mix the veal, half the Parmesan, the pecorino, parsley, ricotta and egg together in a bowl. Season with salt and pepper and roll into 12 or 24 even-sized balls, depending on what size you like. At this stage you can refrigerate the meatballs until you're ready to cook (bring back to room temperature first).

Once the tomatoes are cooked, transfer the contents of the roasting tin to a blender or food processor, blend until smooth and pass through a sieve (strainer) back into the pan. Add the passata, bring to a simmer, then stir in the basil.

To cook the meatballs heat the olive oil in a frying pan over a medium heat and add the meatballs in batches – don't overcrowd the pan. Cook until golden brown all over, transferring them to a plate lined with paper towels to drain between batches. Transfer the cooked meatballs to the sauce and cook for 8–10 minutes, or until cooked through.

Serve the meatballs sprinkled with the remaining grated Parmesan, with the pasta of your choice, or with polenta.

Serves 4

These meatballs are a great British classic that's worth the time and effort. It's quite a challenge to make faggots from scratch, but it's rewarding. I've used caul fat here, which you can probably get from your butcher, along with the pig's liver, heart and lung, and the minced (ground) pork belly. The caul fat is not entirely necessary but it helps hold the meatballs together.

I've gone with frozen peas for this dish because good-quality ones are always tender and not starchy, which fresh ones often are – but mainly because they're readily available and cook almost instantly.

250g (9oz) mix of pig's liver, heart and lung, minced (ground); see above
250g (9oz) minced pork belly (ground pork belly); see above
1 onion, finely chopped
1 garlic clove, finely chopped
2 tbsp finely chopped sage
1 pinch ground allspice
200g (7oz) caul fat (optional; see above)
12 slices of smoked streaky bacon, chopped
500ml (17fl oz) dark chicken stock
2 bay leaves
Sea salt and freshly ground black pepper

For the sauce
75g (2½oz) unsalted butter
2 onions, sliced
A few dashes of Worcestershire sauce
1⅔ tbsp balsamic vinegar
400ml (14fl oz) dark chicken stock
300g (10½oz) frozen peas
12 mint leaves, chopped

Put the minced (ground) pig's liver, heart, lung and pork belly with the onion, garlic, sage and allspice in a bowl and mix until well combined. Season with salt and pepper and shape into 12 even-sized balls, 3 per portion.

Wrap the faggots in one layer of caul fat, if using, then wrap the balls in sliced bacon, one strip per ball. Place the faggots into a deep roasting dish. Cover and chill in the fridge for 30 minutes. They need this time to firm up, so they don't collapse while cooking.

Preheat the oven to 180°C/160°C fan/350°F/gas mark 4.

Pour the chicken stock into the roasting dish so it comes three-quarters of the way up the faggots. Add the bay leaves and poach in the oven for 1 hour, turning every so often, until the faggots are soft and glazed.

To make the sauce, heat 25g (1oz) of the butter in a pan over a medium heat. When hot, add the onion and cook, stirring, for around 10 minutes until soft but not coloured, then add the Worcestershire sauce, vinegar and the stock. Turn up the heat and bring to the boil. Cook for 10–15 minutes, or until the sauce has reduced and thickened to your liking.

Five minutes before the end of the cooking time, add the peas to the sauce and stir in the remaining butter to glaze. Taste and season with salt and pepper.

Just before serving, add the chopped mint to the sauce. Spoon the cooked faggots into a warmed serving bowl and pour over the sauce.

Sunday Lunch

PORK LOIN WITH APPLE, MINT AND CASHEW SALAD

Serves 4

This pork loin on the bone makes a great light Sunday lunch as it is served with a salad rather than roast potatoes. Whenever possible, always try to buy free-range pork with a good layer of fat – the all-important crisp crackling will be much easier to achieve with quality pork.

2kg (4lb 8oz) pork loin on the
  bone, skin on
Olive oil
Juice of 1 lime
Sea salt and freshly ground
  blackpepper

**For the carrot, mint and
cashew salad**
1 eating apple, unpeeled, cored
  and thinly sliced
1 carrot, peeled and thinly sliced
½ cucumber, seeds removed and
  thinly sliced
1 tbsp finely chopped flat
  leaf parsley
1 tbsp finely chopped mint
150g (5½oz) salted cashews,
  toasted and roughly chopped

For the dressing
2 garlic cloves, peeled
  and crushed
2.5cm (1in) piece root ginger,
  peeled and finely grated
1 small red Thai chilli, deseeded
  and finely chopped
2 tbsp palm sugar
4 tbsp lime juice
4 tbsp fish sauce

Before you start cooking take the pork out of the fridge and bring up to room temperature. Preheat the oven to 220°C/200°C fan/425°F/gas mark 7.

Score the skin of the pork all over using the tip of a sharp knife and rub with olive oil and some salt and pepper. Lay the meat skin-side up in a roasting tin.

Put the pork in the oven and blast for 30 minutes. Remove from the oven and squeeze the lime juice all over the skin. Carry on cooking the pork for another 30–45 minutes. Remove from the oven and leave to rest for at least 30 minutes before carving.

Meanwhile, for the carrot, mint and cashew salad, toss all of the ingredients together in a large bowl and set aside.

For the dressing, stir all the ingredients together and taste. Dilute with just enough water to suit your own palate. It should be sharp, sweet, hot and salty, all in equal measure. Spoon the dressing over the salad just before serving and mix well.

When you're ready to eat, remove the crackling and break it into shards. Carve the pork and serve with the salad and crackling pieces.

Serves 2

This is very much in the vein of a Provence-style puff pastry 'pizza'. Light and savoury, it forms a great base for beautifully roasted lamb. I've used the rack here, which admittedly is the most expensive cut, but occasionally it's worth pushing the boat out. A great alternative would be rump of lamb – full of flavour, great texture and delicious crisp fat.

For the tart
250g (9oz) ready-rolled
    puff pastry
25g (1oz) unsalted butter
2 onions, thinly sliced
4 anchovy fillets
150g (5½oz) pitted black
    olives, chopped
2 tbsp olive oil
Juice of 1 lemon
Sea salt and freshly ground
    black pepper

For the lamb
2 tbsp olive oil
1 x 8-bone lamb rack
1 large rosemary sprig
1 garlic clove, smashed

For the port reduction
150ml (5fl oz) ruby port
300ml (10½fl oz) lamb stock
2 tbsp olive oil
1 tomato, deseeded and chopped
2 tbsp finely chopped
    flatleaf parsley

Preheat the oven to 200°C/180°C fan/400°F/gas mark 6.

Cut out 2 x 12cm (4½in) circles from the pastry and place on a baking tray lined with baking paper. Pierce the circles repeatedly with the tines of a fork.

Heat the butter in a frying pan over a medium heat and, when hot, add the onions. Cook, stirring, for 20 minutes, or until soft and slightly caramelized.

Put the anchovy fillets and black olives in a small food processor and blend until smooth. Slowly add the olive oil and lemon juice, then taste and season with salt and pepper if necessary. Spread the anchovy paste over the two pastry circles and top with the softened onions. Bake for 15–20 minutes until the pastry is golden and risen. Set the pastry bases aside, keep warm, and leave your oven at 200°C/180°C fan/400°F/gas mark 6.

Meanwhile, heat an ovenproof frying pan (skillet) over a medium heat. When hot, add the oil. Season the lamb well and add to the pan, searing on all sides for a good colour. This will take 4–6 minutes.

Now throw in the rosemary and garlic, transfer to the oven and cook for a further 5–6 minutes (for medium rare). Remove from the oven and set aside on a plate to rest, loosely covered. Keep the same pan on hand to make the port reduction.

Pour the port into the hot frying pan and boil to reduce by half, then add the lamb stock and reduce again by half Just before serving, stir in the olive oil, chopped tomato and parsley.

Ensure the lamb has rested for at least 10 minutes, then slice the rack into cutlets to serve. Place the tarts on warmed plates to serve, top with the lamb cutlets and spoon over the port sauce.

Sunday Lunch

FIVE-SPICE ROAST GOOSE

Serves 4–6

1 x 5–7kg (11–15lb) whole goose
2 tbsp five-spice powder
1 star anise
1 tsp coriander seeds
3 cloves
Pinch of ground ginger
2 bay leaves
2 heads of garlic
1 bunch of thyme (reserve
    a few sprigs for later)
2 onions, roughly chopped
2 celery sticks, roughly chopped
568ml (20fl oz) water
3 tbsp runny honey
1 tbsp thyme leaves

Goose is a pricey bird but well worth it. It really is for a special occasion and if, like me, you love delicious, crispy skin, then you won't be disappointed. It's a very rich, dense, dark meat, so a little goes a long way. The other benefit is that it yields lots of goose fat, which can be used for all the roast potatoes to come! I've used five-spice rub here because it's my go-to, but a simple sea salt and black pepper mix is still delicious.

Bring the goose to room temperature by taking it out the fridge for a few hours before starting. This is important so the meat doesn't end up being tough. Using a fork, prick the bird all over, especially around the base, legs and thighs.

Using a spice grinder or pestle and mortar, grind the five-spice powder with the star anise, coriander seeds, cloves and ground ginger until you have a fine powder. Rub this powder all over the bird. This can be done a few hours in advance, while the goose is coming to room temperature or the day beforehand.

Put the bay leaves, garlic and bunch of thyme inside the bird. Preheat the oven to 220°C/200°C fan/425°F/gas mark 7.

Put the onions, celery and water in the base of a large roasting tin and place the bird on a wire rack on top. Using a rack will stop the excess fat that drains off from filling the oven with smoke.

Roast for around 30 minutes, then turn the oven temperature down to 180°C/160°C fan/350°F/gas mark 4 and cook for a further 2 hours. Remove from the oven and brush the bird all over with the honey, sprinkle over the thyme leaves and turn the heat back up to 220°C/200°C fan/425°F/gas mark 7 for 20 minutes more to colour and glaze. Remove the bird and allow to rest, covered, for at least 30 minutes before carving. I'd serve this with roasted apples, baby potatoes and watercress.

You'll be left with well over a pint of goose fat. Decant the fat into a clean jar and store in the fridge. It will keep for a long time and is perfect for roasting potatoes and other vegetables.

ROAST RIB OF BEEF WITH YORKSHIRE PUDDING, ONION GRAVY AND CHIVE AND BLACK PEPPER BUTTER

Serves 6–8

Sundays are made special with a rib of beef. For me, a rib is the perfect cut: a good amount of delicious fat, great marbled meat, bones you can chew – basically everything I want in a piece of meat. If you're going to the expense and effort, make sure you visit a good butcher and tell them you want a well sourced, nicely hung piece of meat on the bone.

Meat cooks much better on the bone, but if it comes wrapped in butcher's string, I suggest you cut it off, because it seems to constrict the muscles too much and does nothing to help the end result.

For the roast rib of beef
4 tbsp olive oil
1.5kg (3lb 5oz) rib of beef
1 head of garlic, cut
   in half horizontally
1 small bunch of thyme
3½ tbsp Madeira wine
30g (1oz) salted butter
Sea salt and freshly ground
   black pepper

Right, let's cook the beef. Season the beef well on both sides with salt and pepper – a few hours in advance if you can, otherwise not to worry. Get a large frying pan (skillet) scorching hot and add some oil (use a pan that is ovenproof). Put the beef flat-side down in the pan to colour, then turn over and do the same on the other side. This will take a good 5–10 minutes on each side. Do the same with the fatty part of the meat, holding it down on the base of the hot pan to render the fat and make it crisp.

For the Yorkshire pudding
500g (1lb 2oz) plain
   (all-purpose) flour
1 heaped tsp sea salt
500ml (17fl oz) medium free-
   range eggs (this will be 5–6
   eggs, depending on size)
500ml (17fl oz) milk
Vegetable oil/duck fat or
   goose fat, for cooking the
   Yorkshire puddings

Add the garlic and thyme to the pan with the beef and transfer it to the hot oven. Cook to your preference. It will take 40–45 minutes for medium rare; add about 10–12 minutes on for each desired level of 'doneness'.

When the pan comes out the oven, add the Madeira and use a wooden spoon to scrape up any browned bits from the base of the pan, then whisk in the butter. Baste the meat in these juices, then let it rest, covered, for at least 30 minutes before slicing.

For the onion gravy
30g (1oz) salted butter
1 tbsp olive oil
4 onions, sliced
1 tbsp plain (all-purpose) flour
500ml (17fl oz) red wine
1½ litres (52fl oz) beef stock

Continued overleaf

Sunday Lunch

**For the chive and black
pepper butter**
150g (5½oz) salted butter,
    at room temperature
1 bunch chives, finely chopped
10–15g (¼–½oz) freshly cracked
    black pepper

Meanwhile, for the Yorkshire pudding, put a large roasting tin in the oven to heat up. You can use an individual bun tray, but I prefer one large single Yorkshire pudding, so it is crisp on the edges and soft in the middle.

Put the flour and salt in a large bowl. Make a well in the centre. Mix the eggs with the milk in a jug and pour slowly into the centre, whisking well to prevent lumps. If you do have lumps, just pass the mixture through a sieve (strainer) back into the bowl.

Season with a bit more with salt and pepper, if you like. I've seen mustard and herbs and all sorts of tricks added to the batter at this point, but I don't feel the need, personally. Let the batter stand and rest in the fridge for 30 minutes. This is important as it allows the gluten in the flour to rest.

When ready to cook, pour about 5mm (¼in) of oil or fat into the roasting tin – use duck or goose fat if that's your thing. Shut the oven door and heat the fat up for 5–10 minutes. Now pour the batter in... it should immediately bubble and spit. This is perfect. Pour all the batter into the tin and quickly shut the oven door. Heat and speed are essential here. Now leave it alone (no opening the oven door) and watch it rise. Cook for 25–30 minutes, or until golden and risen. It's a thing of beauty!

To make the onion gravy, heat the butter and oil in a large saucepan over a medium heat. When hot, add the onions and cook, stirring, for 20–30 minutes until they start to brown – the longer the better, to be honest. When you're happy, add the flour and stir into the onions. Cook for 2 minutes. Pour in the wine and cook, stirring, to reduce by half. Finally, add the stock and cook to reduce by half again. Taste and season. Keep warm.

You can make the chive and black pepper butter well ahead of time: put the ingredients in a bowl and mix well, retaining some chives to sprinkle over when serving, if you like. Roll into a log on a piece of baking paper, wrap and chill in the fridge to firm up.

When everything is ready to serve, slice the rested beef and place on a warmed serving plate. If you made a single large Yorkshire pudding, cut it into pieces and place alongside. Serve with the onion gravy and slices of the chive and black pepper butter.

HASSELBACK POTATOES

Serves 4

My absolute favourite way to make the humble potato more interesting – these are crispy on the outside and soft in the middle. You can use butter, goose or duck fat, or even thin strips of lardo or pork fat. These potatoes celebrate the lot!

4 small to medium baking
    potatoes, or 16 new
    potatoes, unpeeled
100g (3½oz) salted butter, softened
100ml (3½fl oz) olive oil
1 tbsp chopped chives (optional)
Sea salt and freshly ground
    black pepper

Set the oven to 220°C/200°C fan/425°F/gas mark 7.

Hold each potato upright lengthways and stick a metal or wooden skewer lengthways through the bottom quarter of each potato. Holding the potato upright with the skewer at the bottom, use a sharp knife to cut down, until you hit the skewer. Repeat, cutting through each spud at regular, narrow intervals (about 3–5mm/⅛–¼in). Remove the skewers.

Sit the potatoes in a pan of cold water for 30 minutes to remove some of the starch and allow the slices to swell a little and separate.

Place the potatoes, cut-side up, on a roasting tray and spread over the butter generously. Drizzle over the olive oil and season well with plenty of salt and pepper. Roast in the oven for around 1 hour, basting frequently.

Serve hot, scattered with the chives, if using.

PAN-ROASTED CARROTS WITH STICKY SHERRY DRESSING, TOASTED ALMONDS AND MANCHEGO CHEESE

Serves 2
generously

Carrots are seen as unexciting, but investing a bit of time, effort and cheese into the proceedings can transform them into the star of the show. The sherry caramel is a great addition and will keep for a few weeks in a sealed jar in the fridge. It goes brilliantly with roasted scallops and a celeriac purée.

350g (12oz) young carrots
125g (4½oz) caster
   (superfine) sugar
4 tbsp amontillado or fino sherry
Sea salt and freshly ground
   black pepper
50g (1¾oz) Manchego cheese,
   to serve

For the toasted almonds
1 tbsp olive oil
25g (1oz) whole blanched almonds
Pinch of sea salt
Pinch of hot smoked paprika

For the dressing
1 tbsp sherry vinegar
3 tbsp olive oil
1 garlic clove, finely chopped

First, scrub the carrots well and dry them, but don't peel them. Heat a dry frying pan (skillet) over a medium heat and add the carrots. Put another pan on top, weighted down with tins. Cook, turning occasionally, for 6–8 minutes depending on the thickness of the carrots. When the carrots are just cooked, turn off the heat and keep them warm in the pan.

Meanwhile, put the caster (superfine) sugar in a dry pan and heat until it turns a golden caramel colour all over, about 5–10 minutes. Tip the pan carefully from side to side as it colours but don't stir. As soon as the sugar takes on a uniform golden caramel appearance, carefully pour in the sherry. It will spit, splutter and possibly ignite so be very careful, and wear oven gloves. When the spluttering calms down, remove from the heat, keep warm and set aside.

To make the toasted almonds, heat the olive oil in a small frying pan, then add the almonds and toast until golden. Sprinkle over the sea salt and smoked paprika. Set aside.

Whisk all the ingredients for the dressing together in a bowl, seasoning with salt and pepper to taste.

To serve, put the pan-roasted carrots in a warmed serving dish and drizzle over the sherry caramel and the dressing. Shave over the Manchego cheese and sprinkle with the toasted almonds.

It's not just the kids who look forward to the desserts. I am unashamedly open about my sweet tooth. Even if I'm too full for a pudding, I can still manage a couple of madeleines (or three) with coffee.

It was tricky to try to narrow down my favourite end-of-meal treats, so in the end I went for the recipes I thought would have the biggest impact without too much effort, with a couple of quirky options thrown in for good measure.

Don't count the calories – it's the weekend!

Desserts

HAZELNUT AND RASPBERRY TORTE WITH CHOCOLATE AND ALMOND CREAM

Serves 8–12

A great combination of rich, decadent chocolate, fresh fruity raspberries and the crunchy bite from the hazelnuts. A really special dessert to round off the evening.

For the torte
200g (7oz) salted butter, softened, plus extra for greasing
175g (6oz) caster (superfine) sugar
3 medium free-range eggs
80g (2½oz) hazelnuts, whizzed to a crumb consistency, plus 100g (3½oz) hazelnuts, roughly chopped
125g (4½oz) plain (all-purpose) flour
1½ tsp baking powder
3–4 tbsp full-fat (whole) milk
300g (10½oz) fresh raspberries
150g (5½oz) dark chocolate, at least 70% cocoa, broken into small pieces

For the chocolate cream
130g (4¾oz) almond butter
100g (3½oz) unsalted butter, softened
130g (4¾oz) icing (confectioners') sugar
80g (2¾oz) cocoa powder
4 tsp–5 tbsp full-fat (whole) milk, to loosen

Preheat the oven to 190°C/170°C fan/375°F/gas mark 5, and grease and line a 23cm (9in) springform cake tin with butter.

To make the torte, beat the butter and sugar in the bowl of a stand mixer or in a large mixing bowl using a hand-held electric whisk for about 10 minutes until pale and soft.

Gradually add the eggs, one by one and mixing between additions, then add the hazelnut crumb, flour and baking powder and mix well. The mixture should have a soft, spoonable consistency. If it is a bit stiff, loosen with the milk (you may not need it all).

Scatter half the fresh raspberries over the bottom of the cake tin (reserve the other half to serve). Pour the cake mixture over the raspberries in the base of the tin and scatter over the chocolate pieces and the chopped hazelnuts. Bake for 1–1½ hours (a skewer inserted into the centre will come out clean when it is done). Take the torte out of the oven and leave on a wire rack to cool.

While the torte is cooking, make the chocolate cream: in a mixing bowl, use a hand-held electric whisk to whisk the almond butter with the butter and sugar until well mixed. Stir in the cocoa powder and just enough milk to loosen to a whipped cream consistency. Keep somewhere cool until ready to serve.

Slice the torte and serve with the chocolate cream and the remaining fresh raspberries.

APRICOT LINZER TORTE

Serves 10–12

This is my take on a classic, lattice-topped tart that can be found in every bakery throughout Austria: delicious crumbly pastry with a sweet, jam-filled middle. I prefer to use apricot jam rather than the traditional redcurrant because it is a touch sweeter. This makes for a very impressive centrepiece.

175g (6oz) plain (all-purpose) flour, plus extra for dusting
Pinch of ground cinnamon
Pinch of ground cloves
40g (1½oz) caster (superfine) sugar
115g (4oz) unsalted butter, softened
2 medium free-range egg yolks, beaten
380g (13½oz) apricot jam (jelly)
6 tbsp raspberry jam (jelly)
Zest and juice of ½ lemon
8–12 whole blanched almonds

To serve
2 tbsp icing (confectioners') sugar (optional)
Custard or single (light) cream

To make the pastry, put the flour, spices and sugar in a mixing bowl. Rub in the butter using your fingertips until the mixture has the consistency of breadcrumbs. Add the egg yolks, mixing well with a wooden spoon to just bring the pastry dough together.

Alternatively you can put the flour, spices and sugar in a food processor, then add the egg yolks and pulse to bring the pastry dough together.

Wrap the dough in cling film (plastic wrap) and chill for at least 1 hour in the fridge.

Preheat the oven to 180°C/160°C fan/350°F/gas mark 4.

Cut off one third of the chilled pastry and set aside to make the lattice top.

Lightly dust the work surface with flour and roll out the larger piece of pastry to a 3mm (⅛in) thickness and use it to line a 23–25cm (9–10in) tart tin.

Make the lattice for the top by rolling out the reserved pastry on a floured surface to a 3mm (⅛in) thickness. Cut it into 12 strips of 25cm (10in) long and about 1cm (½in) wide.

Use the apricot jam (jelly) to fill the pastry case and lay the pastry strips over the top one by one to form a neat lattice pattern. Trim the edges.

Put the raspberry jam in a bowl with the lemon zest and juice, mix well, then transfer to a piping bag fitted with a plain nozzle.

Pipe the jam into alternate squares of the lattice top. On each square of the lattice now filled with jam, place a blanched almond for decoration.

Bake for 25–30 minutes, or until the pastry is crisp and golden brown. Leave to cool in the tin.

If you want to add a pretty touch for serving, dust the torte with icing (confectioners') sugar. Serve sliced with homemade custard or single (light) cream.

Desserts

AUTUMN FRUIT AND ALMOND TART

Serves 10–12

A great, late-summer and autumn dessert. It's soft-centred and really fruity, with a deliciously chewy topping. If you can get hold of them, black figs are far superior in taste to the blander green ones.

For the almond paste
100g (3½oz) unsalted butter, softened
100g (3½oz) caster (superfine) sugar
2 medium free-range eggs, beaten
100g (3½oz) ground almonds

For the apple filling
1kg (2lb 4oz) Bramley apples (or similar cooking apples), peeled and roughly chopped
150g (5½oz) soft light brown sugar
1 tbsp vanilla extract
3½ tbsp apple juice
Juice of 1 lemon

For the topping and tart
1 medium free-range egg white, lightly whisked
25g (1oz) flaked almonds
100g (3½oz) icing (confectioners') sugar
320g (11oz) good-quality shop-bought shortcrust pastry (or see page 155 for homemade)
12 black figs, sliced
400g (14oz) clotted cream or vanilla ice cream, to serve

To make the almond paste, beat together the butter and sugar in a mixing bowl using a hand-held electric whisk until smooth. Slowly add the beaten eggs and stir in the ground almonds. Cover and put it in the fridge to chill while you make the tart.

Next, put the apples, sugar, vanilla extract, apple juice and lemon juice in a pan over a medium heat and cook down to a purée. This will take 15–20 minutes. Add more sugar or lemon juice, to taste.

Preheat the oven to 190°C/170°C fan/375°F/gas mark 5.

For the topping, mix the egg white, flaked almonds and icing (confectioners') sugar together in a bowl.

Roll out the pastry to ½cm (¼in) thickness, and use it to line a 23cm (9in) tart tin, making sure you press the pastry into the base and sides of the tin. Leave an overhang of pastry around the edge – this will be trimmed after it's cooked. Prick the base of the pastry with a fork. Place in the fridge for at least an hour to rest.

Preheat the oven to 180°C/160°C fan/350°F/gas mark 4.

Line the tin with baking paper and fill with baking beans or dried rice or lentils.

Bake in the oven for 20–25 minutes. Remove from the oven and remove the paper and beans. Place back in the oven for 10–15 minutes, or until the pastry is cooked and golden brown. Allow to cool and trim around the edge of the tin using a sharp vegetable peeler or small knife.

To pull it all together, layer the almond paste into the blind-baked pastry shell. Add the apple filling and layer over the fig slices. Dollop the flaked almond topping mixture on top, leaving gaps so you can see the figs. Bake in the oven for 20–30 minutes, or until golden brown and cooked through.

Slice the tart and serve with spoonfuls of clotted cream or vanilla ice cream.

CHERRY, STRAWBERRY AND LEMON GALETTE

Serves 8

This galette makes use of the best soft fruit of the summer season. Always try to buy your fruit a few days before you want to eat it, to give it time to fully ripen — and never tuck it away in the fridge. It may last longer, but it never tastes as good.

For the pastry
200g (7oz) plain (all-purpose) flour, plus extra for dusting
50g (1¾oz) soft light brown sugar
Zest of 1 lemon
125g (4½oz) unsalted butter, diced
4 tbsp very cold water
1 medium free-range egg yolk, beaten
100g (3½oz) ground almonds

For the fruit filling
500g (1lb 2oz) cherries, half pitted, half left whole with stalk attached
300g (10½oz) strawberries, hulled, some quartered and some left whole with the leaves attached
2 tbsp soft light brown sugar
Pared peel of 1 lemon
1 vanilla pod (vanilla bean), seeds removed and pod kept*
1 cinnamon stick (about 8cm/3in)
1 tbsp cornflour (cornstarch)

For the sauce
100g (3½oz) fresh strawberries, hulled
300g (10½oz) fresh cherries, pitted
1 tbsp cherry liqueur

For the cream
150g (5½oz) cream cheese
50g (1¾oz) mascarpone
½ vanilla pod, seeds removed*
50g (1¾oz) icing (confectioners') sugar
50ml (1¾fl oz) double (heavy) cream

Preheat the oven to 220°C/200°C fan/425°F/gas mark 7. To make the pastry, place the flour, sugar and lemon zest in a large bowl. Rub in the butter with your fingers until the mixture resembles breadcrumbs. Slowly add the water and mix until the dough comes together (you may not need all the water). Wrap and leave to rest for 30 minutes in the fridge.

Lightly flour a work surface and roll out the pastry into a circle about 30cm (12in) in diameter and 3mm (⅛in) thick.

For the fruit filling, put the cherries, strawberries, sugar, lemon peel, vanilla seeds and pod, cinnamon and cornflour (cornstarch) in a large bowl and stir to combine. Leave to infuse for about an hour at room temperature.

Meanwhile, for the sauce, put the strawberries, cherries and cherry liqueur in a saucepan over a medium heat and cook until the fruit is soft, about 5 minutes.

Allow to cool slightly, then blend in a food processor until smooth. Pass through a fine sieve (strainer) and pour back into the saucepan. Set aside.

Next, whip the cream cheese, mascarpone, vanilla and icing (confectioners') sugar in a bowl until smooth, by hand or using a hand-held electric whisk. Pour in the double (heavy) cream and stir until combined, but do not whisk further at this stage. Transfer to the fridge and keep covered until ready to serve.

To assemble the galette, remove and discard the vanilla pod,* cinnamon stick and lemon peel from the bowl of fruit filling.

Brush the pastry circle with the beaten egg and place the fruit in the centre of the pastry. Pinch the edges over the fruit to partially enclose and create a pastry case, so the fruit does not spill out. Sprinkle the ground almonds over the top of the fruit filling, but not on the pastry.

Bake in the oven for 30–40 minutes, or until the pastry is golden and the fruit is bubbling. Cut the galette into portions and serve with generous dollops of sauce and cream.

* You could always place the vanilla pod (vanilla bean) in a jar of sugar to have delicious vanilla sugar for the next time you bake.

Serves 6–8

This is actually more of a semifreddo, so you should remove it from the freezer about 15 minutes before serving so that it's slightly softer. I know glacé cherries are a bit retro but apparently we still eat more of them in the UK than anywhere else in the world!

Flavourless vegetable oil,
  for greasing
125g (4½oz) caster
  (superfine) sugar
4 tbsp water
2 medium free-range egg whites
30g (1oz) unsalted pistachios,
  finely chopped
50g (1¾oz) chopped candied peel
30g (1oz) mix of green and red
  glacé (maraschino) cherries,
  finely chopped
2 tbsp sultanas (golden raisins),
  soaked in warm water and
  drained once plump
250ml (9fl oz) double
  (heavy) cream

For the roasted fruits

1 quince, peeled and cut into
  small chunks
2 pears, unpeeled and cut into
  12 slices
1 vanilla pod (vanilla bean),
  split, seeds removed, and
  pod retained
100ml (3½fl oz) runny honey
150ml (5fl oz) Marsala wine
150g (5½oz) blackberries

Grease a 450g (1lb) loaf tin, approximately 24½ x 10cm (9½ x 4in), with a little oil and line it with cling film (plastic wrap).

Put the sugar and water in a small saucepan along with a sugar thermometer and bring to the boil. Once the sugar and water mixture reaches 120°C (248°F), keep at this temperature until needed. Beware, it's not long!

Whisk the egg whites in the bowl of a stand mixer (or in a large mixing bowl using a hand-held electric whisk) until they hold soft peaks.

Keep whisking and gradually pour in the hot sugar syrup, bit by bit, while the mixer is running. Be careful not to pour the syrup directly onto the whisks but into the mixture in the bowl. Keep whisking until the meringue mixture is cool to the touch, about 10 minutes.

Fold into the meringue the pistachios, candied peel, glacé (maraschino) cherries and the soaked and drained sultanas (golden raisins).

Whisk the double (heavy) cream in a separate large mixing bowl using a hand-held electric whisk until the cream will hold soft peaks. Fold the whipped cream into the meringue mix and pour into the lined loaf tin. Cover and freeze until it's set (a minimum of 6 hours).

For the roasted fruits, preheat the oven to 200°C/180°C fan/400°F/gas mark 6. Throw the quince, pear, vanilla seeds (vanilla bean) and pod, honey and Marsala into a roasting tray and mix well. Cook in the oven for 25 minutes. Add the blackberries and cook for a further 5 minutes. Remove the vanilla pod.

If there's any liquid left in the bottom of the roasting tray, strain and transfer to a small saucepan and reduce over a high heat until it has a syrup consistency, then allow to cool.

To serve, remove the cassata from the freezer 15 minutes before you want to serve it. Slice and serve alongside the roasted fruits, drizzled with the syrup, if using.

Desserts

COFFEE, RUM AND RAISIN NO-CHURN ICE CREAM

**Makes just
over 1 litre
(35fl oz)**

110g (3¾oz) raisins
70ml (2¼fl oz) good-quality
   dark rum
1 x 397g (14oz) tin condensed milk
600ml (21fl oz) double
   (heavy) cream
4 tbsp Camp Chicory
   & Coffee Essence
Shot of hot, strong espresso
   or a slug more rum

Super-easy, and no expensive machinery required. The
sugar in the condensed milk prevents the cream from
setting too solidly, but it's a good idea to take the ice cream
out of the freezer a good 5–10 minutes before serving.
The Camp Chicory & Coffee Essence used here is a little
nod to my 1970s upbringing, and it works brilliantly!

Put the raisins in a bowl, add 50ml (3½ tablespoons) of the
dark rum and leave to soak for at least 1 hour.

After 1 hour, mix the condensed milk with the rum-soaked
raisins and the remaining rum.

In a separate bowl whisk the double (heavy) cream until
it forms soft peaks and stir in the Camp Chicory & Coffee
Essence. Freeze overnight in a sealed container.

To serve, scoop the ice cream into a serving bowl. Serve
with the shot of hot, strong espresso or rum poured over
the top, depending on the time of day or your mood!

The ice cream will keep in the freezer for up to 1 month.

BABY PINEAPPLES WITH FROZEN GREEK YOGHURT

Serves 4

Quite a dessert this one, an interesting combination of sweet sticky caramel, juicy warm pineapple, spicy ginger and hot chilli. I absolutely love it, and looks great as a centrepiece.

For the frozen Greek yoghurt
400g (14oz) full-fat thick
    Greek yoghurt
40g (1½oz) caster
    (superfine) sugar
Juice of 1 lime
6 mint leaves, thinly sliced

For the roasted baby pineapples
400g (14oz) caster
    (superfine) sugar
200ml (7fl oz) dark rum
1 star anise
2 x 5cm (2in) cinnamon sticks
2 vanilla pods (vanilla beans),
    split and seeds removed,
    reserve the pods
1 red chilli, deseeded
    and chopped
4cm (1½in) piece root ginger,
    peeled and grated
4 lime leaves, thinly sliced
Juice of 2 limes
4 baby pineapples, peeled and
    cored, tops reserved

For the frozen Greek yoghurt, put the yoghurt in a large mixing bowl with the sugar and lime juice and whisk thoroughly. Fold through the mint leaves.

Transfer the mixture to an ice cream machine and churn, following the manufacturer's instructions, until smooth. Transfer to a sealed container and put in the freezer for a good 3 hours, until solid.

Preheat the oven to 160°C/140°C fan/320°F/gas mark 3.

Heat a medium sauté pan over a medium heat. Sprinkle the sugar over the base of the pan and cook until a caramel is formed, gently tipping the pan carefully from side to side as the sugar cooks, but do not stir. The caramel is ready when the surface has a uniform golden colour.

Carefully add the dark rum, wearing oven gloves to protect your hands, as the mixture might spit. Add the star anise, cinnamon sticks, vanilla seeds and reserved pods, chilli, ginger, lime leaves and lime juice. At this stage, you can stir the caramel and flavourings together using a wooden spoon.

Place the pineapples in a small roasting dish and pour over the warm caramel. Cover the pineapples with foil and cook for about 1 hour, basting the pineapples with the caramel several times as they cook. They are ready when you can push a metal skewer into the centre without much resistance.

Remove the pineapples from the oven. Place the reserved green tops back on top of each pineapple and serve with the frozen Greek yoghurt.

MADELEINES

Makes 24

These often make an appearance after a big, long lunch in our house instead of dessert. They are best served fresh from the oven and still warm. If you want to step them up a gear, some really good lemon curd goes well with them, as does a little crème fraîche and honey.

I often find that anyone who complains that they are too full for dessert often manages to destroy a pile of madeleines without hesitation.

2 large free-range eggs
125g (4½oz) caster
   (superfine) sugar
125g (4½oz) salted butter
Juice of ½ lemon
75g (2½oz) plain
   (all-purpose) flour
35g (1¼oz) cornflour (cornstarch)
Pinch of salt
Pinch of freshly grated nutmeg
Icing (confectioners') sugar,
   to serve

Using a hand-held electric whisk, whisk the eggs and sugar in a bowl until light and thick, about 10 minutes.

Melt the butter in a saucepan, swirling the pan until the butter is melted and is evenly nut brown in colour. Immediately add the lemon juice, then take the pan off the heat and let the butter cool a little.

In a separate bowl, combine the flour, cornflour (cornstarch), salt and nutmeg.

Carefully fold the flour mixture into the egg and sugar mixture, then pour in the melted browned butter and lemon juice. Allow the batter to stand for at least 30 minutes.

Preheat the oven to 200°C/180°C fan/400°F/gas mark 6. Grease two 12-hole non-stick madeleine trays. Pour the batter evenly among the holes and cook for 10–12 minutes until risen and golden.

Allow the madeleines to cool for 10 minutes before tipping out of the trays. Pile high on a serving plate. Dust with icing (confectioners') sugar and serve while still warm.

FLORENTINES

Makes 25

90g (3¼oz) salted butter
160g (5¾oz) caster
   (superfine) sugar
230ml (7¼fl oz) double
   (heavy) cream
250g (9oz) flaked almonds
200g (7oz) blanched hazelnuts,
   toasted in a dry pan
150g (5½oz) stem ginger, chopped
80g (2¾oz) raisins
20g (¾oz) plain (all-purpose) flour

Nutty and chewy with a toffee-like sweetness, these little Italian beauties are one of my all-time favourites. (Pictured overleaf.)

Preheat the oven to 200°C/180°C fan/400°F/gas mark 6. Line 2 baking trays with baking paper.

Bring the butter, sugar and cream to the boil in a saucepan over a medium heat, stirring until the sugar is dissolved. Add the rest of the ingredients and stir together off the heat.

Spoon the mixture onto the trays, leaving about 5cm (2in) between each one to allow for spreading during cooking. Bake for around 8 minutes, or until they look golden and lacy. Remove from the oven and allow the florentines to cool fully before attempting to carefully lift them off the trays, as they will be quite fragile.

Makes 16–18

150g (5½oz) whole blanched
    almonds, toasted in a dry pan
    and chopped
260g (9¼oz) soft light brown sugar
160g (5¾oz) plain
    (all-purpose) flour
¼ tsp baking powder
1 tsp lemon juice

These actually do look like lifeless fingers. Despite their appearance, they taste great! (Pictured overleaf.)

Preheat the oven to 190°C/170°C fan/375°F/gas mark 5. Line 2 baking trays with baking paper.

Using your hands, combine the almonds, sugar, flour and baking powder in a mixing bowl, then add the lemon juice. Mix well, pressing together to form a stiff dough.

Roll the dough into 16–18 irregular-shaped fingers about 10cm (4in) long and 1cm (½in) thick.

Bake on the prepared baking trays for around 10 minutes until they look lightly golden. Let them cool on the trays for 10 minutes before removing.

ALMOND BISCUITS

Makes 25–30

These delicious biscuits originate from a small hotel in Puglia that I used to visit. The chef would make them every morning for breakfast and they were the perfect accompaniment to a spoonful of homemade lemon marmalade, freshly made ricotta and a strong espresso. A brilliant combination. (Pictured on page 210.)

500g (1lb 2oz) ground almonds
250g (9oz) icing (confectioners')
    sugar, plus extra for dusting
Zest of 1 lemon
Pinch of salt
2 medium free-range eggs

Mix the ground almonds, icing (confectioners') sugar, lemon zest and salt together in a bowl. Beat the eggs in a jug and slowly add them to the dry ingredients, mixing to form a stiff dough. Roll the dough out on a work surface into a log shape around 4cm (1½in) thick, dusting with the extra icing sugar to prevent sticking.

Chill the dough in the fridge for 30 minutes to firm up.

Preheat the oven to 200°C/180°C fan/400°F/gas mark 6. Line 2 baking trays with baking paper.

Cut the chilled dough into 5mm (¼in) thick rounds and lay them on the lined baking trays. Push down gently with the heel of your hand to flatten them slightly, then bake for 20–25 minutes until lightly golden. Allow to cool for 10 minutes before removing them from the trays.

SUMMER FRUIT FIZZ WITH LEMON BALM

Serves 4

Simple to make but with a touch of theatre, this fresh summer fruit soup makes an easy and impressive end to a great lunch. Substitute other soft fruit if you prefer – a mix of flavours works best. If you have trouble finding the lemon balm, you could use fresh basil leaves instead.

1 bottle of sparkling wine, prosecco, cava or Champagne

For the summer fruit fizz
100g (3½oz) strawberries
100g (3½oz) raspberries
100g (3½oz) blackberries
100g (3½oz) redcurrants
100g (3½oz) blueberries
100g (3½oz) blackcurrants
10 or so mint leaves, shredded
120g (4¼oz) full-fat crème fraîche, to serve

For the syrup
400ml (14fl oz) water
350g (12oz) caster (superfine) sugar
1 lemon, pared into strips of zest and juiced
1 bunch of lemon balm

For the summer fruit fizz, toss all the fruit together in a large bowl with the shredded mint leaves.

To make the syrup, bring the water, sugar, lemon juice and pared zest and the lemon balm leaves to a simmer in a large saucepan. Turn the heat off and allow to steep and cool for 10 minutes.

Pour the syrup over the fruit in the bowl, then leave to macerate for at least 2 hours.

Put the glasses or glass serving bowls into the fridge to chill for 30 minutes or so.

Spoon the fruit and some of the syrup into the chilled glasses or bowls and pour over the sparkling wine (you can use whatever fizz you have).

Serve immediately while still bubbling, with a small dollop of crème fraîche.

ORANGE AND CAMPARI GRANITA 70S-STYLE

Serves 8

A light and refreshing end to a good dinner or a summer lunch, bitter and sweet in equal measure. An adult version of those sorbets you used to get as a kid in Mediterranean restaurants.

8 whole fresh oranges
50g (1¾oz) caster (superfine) sugar
3½ tbsp water
150ml (5fl oz) Campari, plus extra to serve
500ml (17fl oz) orange juice, from the 8 oranges, plus extra juice as needed to make up the quantity

Cut the oranges in half. Using a juicer, press and twist the oranges to release the juice and clean the insides. Strain and reserve the juice. Pull and scrape away any pith and freeze the orange halves.

Put the sugar and water in a pan over a low heat and stir until the sugar is dissolved, about 5 minutes. Pour in the Campari and the orange juice, then tip the mixture into a shallow baking tray and transfer to the freezer. After an hour, take the granita out of the freezer and scrape the surface with a fork.

Keep doing this for a good few hours until the granita is set and granular. (At this stage, the granita will keep in a sealed container in the freezer for up to 3 months.)

Take the granita out of the freezer 5 minutes before serving and fork through.

To serve, spoon the granita into the hollowed-out oranges. Pour a splash of Campari over for an extra kick.

Index

aioli, saffron 129
almond butter: almond and
    yoghurt dressing 116
    chocolate and almond
    cream 194
almonds: almond biscuits 212
    almond paste 198
    apricot and almond pastry
    swirls 53
    dead men's fingers 209
    florentines 208
    granola 54
    toasted almonds 191
Alpine-style stuffed bread 46
American-style Cobb salad 74
anchovies: anchoïade 115
    charred broccoli, ricotta,
    grilled chillies and anchovy
    152
    parsley, tarragon and garlic and
    anchovy sauce 155
    Provence-style tart 183
    sambal 64
apples: apple and fennel salad 88
    apple, mint and cashew salad
    178
    autumn fruit and almond tart
    198
    carrot and apple pickle 73
    spiced roasted apple 169
apricot and almond pastry
    swirls 53
apricot jam: apricot Linzer
    torte 197
asparagus: blackened asparagus
    and chorizo vinaigrette 65
aubergines (eggplant): Puglian
    stuffed aubergine 124
    sea bass wok fish 138
autumn fruit and almond tart 198

avocados: American-style Cobb
    salad 74
    mashed avocado 63
    prawn rolls with avocado 20
    sesame and salted cucumber
    with avocado 78

bacon: crisp bacon and devilled
    eggs 70
    pork faggots 177
    roast winter vegetables with
    Comté cheese and bacon 128
    warm salad of smoked
    haddock, black pudding and
    bacon 69
    see also pancetta
basil: pesto 24–5
bass see sea bass
beans see broad beans,
    cannellini beans etc
béarnaise sauce 144–6
beef: beef and onion pie 155
    beef cheek burgers 112
    biltong 110
    crispy beef tostadas 45
    poached fillet of beef 160–1
    Reuben sandwich 107
    roast rib of beef 185–6
biltong 110
biscuits: almond biscuits 212
    dead men's fingers 209
black pudding: warm salad of
    smoked haddock, black
    pudding and bacon 69
blackberries: blackberry, ricotta
    and citrus pancakes 50
    roasted fruits 201
blueberries, Greek yoghurt
    with 54
bone marrow, gnocchi alla

romana with 158
borlotti beans: minestrone
    soup 168
bread: Alpine-style stuffed
    bread 46
    coconut bread 57
    croutons 128
    Durban bunny chow with
    prawns 40
    flatbreads 36, 63
    Gruyère and ham croutons 166
    harissa toast 168
    za'atar flatbread 143
    see also sandwiches; toast
    bread and butter pickles 107
broad beans: minestrone
    soup 168
broccoli: barbecued broccoli
    with honey and blue cheese
    dressing 96
    charred broccoli, ricotta,
    grilled chillies and anchovy 152
bulgur wheat: citrus parsley
    salad 91
burgers: beef cheek burgers 112
    lentil burgers 73
    pork banh mi 33
butter: béarnaise sauce 144–6
    chive and black pepper butter
    185–6
    hollandaise beurre noisette
    160–1
    seaweed butter 137
buttermilk fried chicken 30–1
buttermilk sauce 102–3
butternut squash roasted with
    pancetta 126

cabbage and caraway 147
cakes: madeleines 206

Campari: orange and Campari granita 70s-style 215
candied peel: cassata ice cream 201
cannellini beans: minestrone soup 168
spiced marinated leg of lamb with white beans 156
Cape Malay lamb curry 38–9
caramel: roasted baby pineapples 204
carrots: apple, mint and cashew salad 178
carrot and apple pickle 73
carrot pickle 33
pan-roasted carrots with sticky sherry dressing 191
cashews: apple, mint and cashew salad 178
toasted quinoa salad 83
cassata ice cream 201
cauliflower: cumin-roasted cauliflower 27
spicy crisp-fried cauliflower 28
cheese: Alpine-style stuffed bread 46
courgette and Parmesan soup 164
crisp-fried goat's cheese with lentils 169
garden salad with goat's cheese 124
gnocchi alla romana 158
Gruyère and ham croutons 166
Gruyère cheese, spinach and nutmeg tart 122–3
honey and blue cheese dressing 96
Mexican-style grilled corn 94
Parmesan fritters with Roquefort spinach 170
pesto 24–5
Reuben sandwich 107
roast butternut squash with pancetta and Gruyère and Parmesan cream 126
roast winter vegetables with Comté cheese and bacon 128
salami, potato and Gruyère cheese 65
warm halloumi with watermelon, Parma ham and herbs 87

whipped feta with blackened spring onions 84
see also mascarpone; ricotta
cherries (glacé): cassata ice cream 201
cherry, strawberry and lemon galette 200
chicken: American-style Cobb salad 74
buttermilk fried chicken 30–1
chicken, ham hock and Jerusalem artichoke pithivier 149
hot and sour soup 16
poached chicken with citrus parsley salad 91
Portuguese chicken, coriander and garlic soup 12
roast chicken with salt-and-vinegar potato chips 144–6
rosemary chicken 29
smoky spring chicken 102–3
chickpeas: grilled vegetables 116
sautéed chilli squid 134
toasted quinoa salad 83
chicory (endive): American-style Cobb salad 74
chillies: charred broccoli, ricotta, grilled chillies and anchovy 152
charred pineapple salsa 30–1
chilli dressing 84
jalapeño salsa 118
pork banh mi with crispy bits 33
sun-dried tomato and chilli toast 101
zhoug dressing 118
chips, salt-and-vinegar potato 144–6
chive and black pepper butter 185–6
chocolate and almond cream 194
chorizo: blackened asparagus and chorizo vinaigrette 65
home-salted cod with chorizo 129
chutney, mint 156
cilantro see coriander
citrus parsley salad 91
clam vinaigrette 174
Cobb salad 74
coconut: granola 54

coconut milk: coconut bread 57
nasi lemak 64
cod: home-salted cod with chorizo 129
coffee, rum and raisin no-churn ice cream 202
coriander (cilantro): Portuguese chicken, coriander and garlic soup 12
slow-cooked lamb with coriander dressing 154
zhoug dressing 118
corn on the cob: jalapeño salsa 118
Mexican-style grilled corn 94
sweetcorn and mango salsa 102–3
corned beef: Reuben sandwich 107
courgette (zucchini) and Parmesan soup 164
couscous, herb 38–9
crab scones 88
crème fraîche: raspberry cream 57
crispy bits, pork banh mi with 33
croquettes, curried potato 72
croutons 128
Gruyère and ham croutons 166
crudités with anchoïade 115
cucumber: bread and butter pickles 107
cucumber and yoghurt 28
cucumber pickle 131
cucumber salad 63
sesame and salted cucumber 78
cumin-roasted cauliflower 27
curry: Cape Malay lamb curry 38–9
curried potato croquettes 72
duck massaman curry 43
Durban bunny chow with prawns 40

dead men's fingers 209
dim sum prawn dumplings 23
dips: anchoïade 115
Sichuan pepper and peanut dip 27
dressings: almond and yoghurt dressing 116
blackened asparagus and chorizo vinaigrette 65

chilli dressing 84
clam vinaigrette 174
coriander dressing 154
ginger and soy dressing 18
honey and blue cheese
 dressing 96
kale vinaigrette 126
piri-piri dressing 83
sesame seed dressing 98
sticky sherry dressing 191
zhoug dressing 118
drinks: orange and Campari
 granita 70s-style 215
 summer fruit fizz with lemon
 balm 213
duck: duck massaman
 curry 43
 duck sausage rolls 109
dumplings: dim sum prawn
 dumplings 23
 malfatti with tuna 24–5
Durban bunny chow with
 prawns 40
Dutch baby with figs and
 raspberries 60

edamame beans: sesame and
 salted cucumber 78
eggplants see aubergines
eggs: crisp bacon and devilled
 eggs 70
 crispy egg 116, 173
 eggs and things 65
 poached eggs 12, 63, 72
endive see chicory

faggots, pork 177
fennel: apple and fennel salad 88
 roast bass with fennel and
 lemon thyme 141
figs: autumn fruit and almond tart
 198
 Dutch baby with figs and
 raspberries 60
five-spice roast goose 184
flatbreads 36, 63
 za'atar flatbread 143
florentines 208
French onion soup 166
fritters, Parmesan 170
fruit: summer fruit fizz with lemon
 balm 213
 see also apples, raspberries etc

galette: cherry, strawberry
 and lemon 200
garden salad 124
garlic: garlic mayonnaise 29
 saffron aioli 129
ginger: florentines 208
 ginger and soy dressing 18
girolles, pickled 137
gnocchi alla romana 158
goat's cheese: crisp-fried goat's
 cheese with lentils 169
 garden salad with goat's
 cheese 124
goose, five-spice roast 184
granita: orange and Campari
 granita 70s-style 215
granola 54
gravy, onion 185–6
Greek yoghurt with blueberries,
 granola and almond butter 54
gremolata 134
Gruyère cheese, spinach and
 nutmeg tart 122–3

haddock see smoked haddock
ham: chicken, ham hock and
 Jerusalem artichoke pithivier
 149
 Gruyère and ham croutons 166
 ham hock and pea purée 173
 warm halloumi with
 watermelon, Parma ham and
 herbs 87
harissa paste: harissa monkfish
 143
 harissa toast 168
hasselback potatoes 188
hazelnuts: florentines 208
 hazelnut and raspberry torte
 194
herb couscous 38–9
hollandaise beurre noisette 160–1
honey and blue cheese dressing
 96
horseradish crust, mackerel
 fillets with 19
hot and sour soup 16
ice cream: cassata ice cream 201
 coffee, rum and raisin no-
 churn ice cream 202

jalapeño salsa 118
jam: apricot Linzer torte 197

raspberry cream 57
Jerusalem artichokes: chicken,
 ham hock and Jerusalem
 artichoke pithivier 149

kale: kale vinaigrette 126
 toasted quinoa salad 83
ketchup, tamarind 119
kidneys, sautéed 158

lamb: Cape Malay lamb curry
 38–9
 Provence-style tart with roast
 lamb 183
 rack of lamb with charred
 broccoli, ricotta, grilled
 chillies and anchovy 152
 salt and pepper lamb
 chops 104
 slow-cooked lamb with
 coriander dressing 154
 spiced lamb flatbread 36
 spiced marinated leg of
 lamb 156
langoustines with sesame seed
 dressing 98
lemon balm, summer fruit fizz
 with 213
lentils: crisp-fried goat's cheese
 with lentils 169
 lentil burgers 73
 toasted quinoa salad 83
liver: pork faggots 177

mackerel fillets with horseradish
 crust 19
madeleines 206
malfatti with tuna 24–5
mangoes: fresh mango salsa 20
 sweetcorn and mango
 salsa 102–3
mascarpone: raspberry cream 57
mayonnaise: garlic
 mayonnaise 29
 mushroom mayo 112
 saffron aioli 129
 sriracha and herb
 mayonnaise 33
meatballs, veal and ricotta 176
Mexican-style grilled corn 94
minestrone soup 168
mint chutney 156
miso butter and shallots 65

monkfish, harissa 143
mushrooms: king scallops with
    pickled girolles 137
    miso mushrooms 29
    mushroom and tarragon
        soup 165
    mushroom mayo 112
    sea bass wok fish 138
mustard cream sauce 149

nasi lemak 64
noodles: salmon, ginger and
    chilli broth 15

oats: granola 54
olives: Provence-style tart 183
onions: beef and onion pie 155
    French onion soup 166
    onion gravy 185–6
    Provence-style tart 183
oranges: orange and Campari
    granita 70s-style 215
    pomegranate and orange
        salad 143
ossi de morti (dead men's
    fingers) 209

pancakes: blackberry, ricotta
    and citrus 50
pancetta: cabbage and
    caraway 147
    roast butternut squash with
        pancetta 126
Parmesan fritters 170
parsley: citrus parsley salad 91
    gremolata 134
    parsley, tarragon and garlic and
        anchovy sauce 155
pastries: apricot and almond
pastry swirls 53
    duck sausage rolls 109
    see also pies; tarts
    pastry 122, 155, 200
peanut butter: peanut and
    sesame sauce 73
    Sichuan pepper and peanut
        dip 27
pears: roasted fruits 201
peas: garden salad 124
    ham hock and pea purée 173
    pork faggots with peas, mint
        and vinegar 177
pecans: granola 54

pesto 24–5
pickles: bread and butter
    pickles 107
    carrot and apple pickle 73
    carrot pickle 33
    cucumber pickle 131
    pickled girolles 137
pies: beef and onion pie 155
    chicken, ham hock and
        Jerusalem artichoke
        pithivier 149
    see also pastries; tarts
pine nuts: pesto 24–5
    Puglian stuffed aubergine 124
pineapple: baby pineapples with
    frozen Greek yoghurt 204
    charred pineapple salsa 30–1
piri-piri dressing 83
pistachios: cassata ice cream 201
pithivier: chicken, ham hock and
    Jerusalem artichoke 149
pomegranate and orange
    salad 143
pork: dim sum prawn
    dumplings 23
    duck sausage rolls 109
    pork banh mi with crispy bits 33
    pork faggots with peas, mint
        and vinegar 177
    pork loin with apple, mint and
        cashew salad 178
port: roast lamb 183
Portuguese chicken, coriander
    and garlic soup 12
potatoes: Alpine-style stuffed
    bread 46
    curried potato croquettes 72
    hasselback potatoes 188
    roast bass with fennel and
        lemon thyme 141
    salami, potato and Gruyère
        cheese 65
    salt-and-vinegar potato chips
        144–6
prawns (shrimp): dim sum prawn
    dumplings 23
    Durban bunny chow with
        prawns 40
    prawn rolls with avocado 20
    sugar-cured prawns 70
    Provence-style tart with roast
        lamb 183
    Puglian stuffed aubergine 124

quince: roasted fruits 201
quinoa: curried potato
    croquettes 72
    toasted quinoa salad and
        piri-piri dressing 83

raisins: coffee, rum and raisin
    no-churn ice cream 202
    florentines 208
    granola 54
raspberries: Dutch baby with figs
    and raspberries 60
    hazelnut and raspberry
        torte 194
raspberry jam: raspberry
    cream 57
ray: sautéed ray wing with clam
    vinaigrette 174
red mullet, roasted 101
Reuben sandwich 107
rice: nasi lemak 64
ricotta: blackberry, ricotta and
    citrus pancakes 50
    charred broccoli, ricotta,
        grilled chillies and
        anchovy 152
    malfatti with tuna 24–5
    veal and ricotta meatballs 176
rosemary chicken 29
rum: coffee, rum and raisin
    no-churn ice cream 202
    roasted baby pineapples 204

saffron aioli 129
salads: American-style Cobb
salad 74
    apple and fennel salad 88
    apple, mint and cashew
        salad 178
    citrus parsley salad 91
    cucumber salad 63
    garden salad 124
    pomegranate and orange
        salad 143
    sesame and salted
        cucumber 78
    toasted quinoa salad and
        piri-piri dressing 83
    warm salad of smoked
        haddock, black pudding
        and bacon 69
    salami, potato and Gruyère
        cheese 65

salmon: salmon, crème fraîche, Dijon and tarragon 65
    salmon, ginger and chilli broth 15
salsa: charred pineapple salsa 30–1
    fresh mango salsa 20
    jalapeño salsa 118
    sweetcorn and mango salsa 102–3
salt and pepper lamb chops 104
salt-and-vinegar potato chips 144–6
sambal 64
sandwich, Reuben 107
sauces: béarnaise sauce 144–6
    buttermilk sauce 102–3
    hollandaise beurre noisette 160–1
    mustard cream sauce 149
    onion gravy 185–6
    parsley, tarragon and garlic and anchovy sauce 155
    peanut and sesame sauce 73
    pesto 24–5
    squid ink sauce 134
    tamarind ketchup 119
    tomato sauce 24–5, 176
    vermouth sauce 19
sauerkraut: Reuben sandwich 107
sausage rolls, duck 109
sausages: Alpine-style stuffed bread 46
    Puglian stuffed aubergine 124
scallops: king scallops with pickled girolles 137
scones, crab 88
sea bass: roast bass with fennel and lemon thyme 141
    sea bass wok fish 138
seaweed butter 137
semolina: gnocchi alla romana 158
sesame seeds: granola 54
    peanut and sesame sauce 73
    sesame and salted cucumber 78
    sesame seed dressing 98
shallots, miso butter and 65
sherry: sticky sherry dressing 191
shrimp see prawns
Sichuan pepper and peanut dip 27
smoked haddock: warm salad of

smoked haddock, black pudding and bacon 69
soups: courgette and Parmesan soup 164
    French onion soup 166
    hot and sour soup 16
    mushroom and tarragon soup 165
    Portuguese chicken, coriander and garlic soup 12
    salmon, ginger and chilli broth 15
    spring minestrone soup 168
spinach: Gruyère cheese, spinach and nutmeg tart 122–3
    malfatti with tuna 24–5
    Roquefort spinach 170
    seared tuna with ginger and soy dressing 18
spring minestrone soup 168
spring onions: whipped feta with blackened spring onions 84
squash see butternut squash
squid: sautéed chilli squid with squid ink sauce 134
    squid toasts 131
sriracha and herb mayonnaise 33
strawberries: cherry, strawberry and lemon galette 200
sugar-cured prawns 70
summer fruit fizz with lemon balm 213
sweetcorn see corn on the cob

tamarind paste: sambal 64
    tamarind ketchup 119
tarragon: béarnaise sauce 144–6
    mushroom and tarragon soup 165
    parsley, tarragon and garlic and anchovy sauce 155
tarts: apricot Linzer torte 197
    autumn fruit and almond tart 198
    cherry, strawberry and lemon galette 200
    Gruyère cheese, spinach and nutmeg tart 122–3
    Provence-style tart 183
    see also pastries; pies
toast: harissa toast 168
    squid toasts 131

sun-dried tomato and chilli toast 101
tomatoes: Cape Malay lamb curry 38–9
    sun-dried tomato and chilli toast 101
    tamarind ketchup 119
    tomato sauce 24–5, 176
tortes: apricot Linzer torte 197
    hazelnut and raspberry torte 194
tortillas: crispy beef tostadas 45
tuna: malfatti with tuna 24–5
    seared tuna with ginger and soy dressing 18

veal: pot-roasted veal 147
    veal and ricotta meatballs 176
vegetables: crudités with anchoïade 115
    grilled vegetables 116
    roast winter vegetables with Comté cheese and bacon 128
    see also peppers, tomatoes etc
vermouth sauce 19
vinaigrette 160–1
    blackened asparagus and chorizo vinaigrette 65
    clam vinaigrette 174
    kale vinaigrette 126

watermelon, warm halloumi with 87
wine: poached fillet of beef 160–1
    slow-cooked lamb with coriander dressing 154
    summer fruit fizz with lemon balm 213
wonton wrappers: dim sum prawn dumplings 23

yoghurt: almond and yoghurt dressing 116
    cucumber and yoghurt 28
    frozen Greek yoghurt 204
    Greek yoghurt with blueberries, granola and almond butter 54
    herbed yoghurt 36
Yorkshire pudding 185–6

za'atar flatbread 143
zhoug dressing 118
zucchini see courgettes

Acknowledgements

Firstly, I'd obviously like to thank my beautiful, long-suffering and patient wife Lisa, and my two massively entertaining yet increasingly expensive kids, Jessie and Henry ... thanks for all the 'constructive' criticism, often unsolicited but sometimes necessary!

All the crew at Cactus, led by the fearless and irrepressible Amanda Ross. They make *Saturday Kitchen* such a great show to work on and allow me to have the time of my life, while dangerously forgetting I'm actually on live TV, week after week. I literally could not ask for a better team.

To my publisher, Sarah Lavelle, and all her fabulous team, who did a brilliant job of steering this ship despite the endless lockdowns and zoom glitches. I couldn't be happier with the results.

My great friend and amazing photographer, Chris Terry, who makes everything look so good through a lens. (But you really need to embrace those iPhone filters kid, it's so much easier!)

My home economist, Michaela, who often gets an unwelcomed mention on the show, but who always puts her bright red lipstick on just before we go live, in case I make her run on stage. It's a fun game to play! Thanks for all the graft on the show and this shoot, I could not have managed without you.

My lovely agents, Hilary and Charlotte, who look after me so well ... although I'm still not sure what they mean by: "Are your diamond shoes too tight Matt?" It's puzzling.

Thank you to Nikki, who introduced me to the very best kitchen suppliers, TPB, Wolf & Sub Zero, Novy, Ox-grills. I couldn't wish for better kit, it makes my kitchen life immeasurably easier, and to Drew at Quails, who fitted it all out so beautifully.

Last, but certainly not least, all my wonderful family and friends who have helped and encouraged me through all the highs and lows, and who set me on the path to the best job I could have wished for.

Cheers to you all and enjoy the weekend!

Publishing Director Sarah Lavelle
Editor Stacey Cleworth
Editorial Assistant Sofie Shearman
Head of Design Claire Rochford
Design and Art Direction Studio Polka
Photographer Chris Terry
Food Stylists Matt Tebbutt and Michaela Bowles
Prop Stylist Faye Wears
Head of Production Stephen Lang
Production Controller Nikolaus Ginelli

Thank you to Davies and Co for providing beautiful
Welsh blankets for this book.

Published in 2021 by Quadrille, an imprint of Hardie Grant Publishing

Quadrille
52–54 Southwark Street
London SE1 1UN
quadrille.com

Cataloguing in Publication Data: a catalogue record for this book
is available from the British Library.

UK ISBN 978 1 78713 753 0
US ISBN 978 1 78713 757 8

Printed in China